Into the Breach

Protect Your Business by Managing People, Information, and Risk

by

Michael J. Santarcangelo II

Praise for *Into the Breach*

"Michael has positioned himself as a leader in the evolution of security, and his book is an invitation to evolve for those who have realized that pumping an ever-increasing sum of money into yet another technology just doesn't make sense. For years, security practitioners and vendors have been touting nothing but electronic solutions—the cure for what ails your organization, be it hackers, viruses, data loss, or audit findings. But they keep forgetting that the technology is only as good as the people who use it. It only takes one well-intended but unaware user to render a multi-million dollar security technology useless. *Into the Breach* is the first book that actually focuses on the foundation of the problem—user awareness. Make your users security-aware, give them an ownership stake in protecting the company's assets, and they will allow your technology implementations to be successful."

Ioana Bazavan Justus, co-author,
Information Security Cost
Management

"This book reveals a radically different approach to the breach problem than anything else you hear and read. It certainly has given me cause to rethink some of the work I am doing in this area. I've read that a number of security problems are caused by employees, but I've never seen anything other than the heavy hammer approach to solving the problem. It was refreshing to see something new."

Richard Spratt, Manager of Data
Privacy and Security,
Sun Microsystems Inc.

"*Into the Breach* breaks down the truth behind information protection. Michael Santarcangelo has done a tremendous job at providing a powerful overview of the human behavior aspect of security in a 3-hour easy read. This is a must-read for all security professionals and business leaders to get a full appreciation for the information protection strategy which consists of three basic parts:

- Understand the information and information resources of the organization.
- Engage, empower, and enable people.
- Optimize process and technology.

Into the Breach can serve as the core for any security education and awareness program that is geared toward changing the behavior of its associates and weaving security into the fabric of an organization. Michael has been able to put onto paper, in a very concise manner, concepts that have helped me over my 23-year career in the security profession."

Scott M. Angelo, CISSP, CISM,
VP, Chief Information
Security Officer

To my children:
I wrote this for you. My hope is that my
generation solves more problems than we
create—allowing you to stand on our shoulders
and do even greater things.

To Tricia:
I could fill a book with the gratitude I feel
for your steadfast belief in me and unending
support. If only others were as lucky to have
what we have in life . . .

To my family:
Not only did you support me through this
journey, but you prepared me for it. And now,
we begin . . .

Acknowledgments

The wisdom of children was at work during the development of this book. As I was about to start a planned weekend writing session—alone, as my family was about to travel—my young son came into my office, in tears. He didn't want to leave me alone for the weekend and asked to stay. He explained that if I was writing a book, he would too. He won the argument, and we printed out pictures for him to color. He received a section of desk to work on, markers and pens to color with, folders for organization, and a bag to hold his entire manuscript. We worked side-by-side all weekend long, with some breaks for eating, hockey, and to watch a few movies. It was only the start of a noble pursuit.

Whenever asked about the status of his book—the effort, of course, took longer than the weekend—he would answer with the same words and candor I offered to the same question. It turned out that we were on the same schedule. I may not have gotten as much writing done that weekend as I had hoped, but what I got in return was far greater. That experience will live with me forever and tempered the approach of this book with his insights and the importance of the human connection.

Somewhere during one of the revisions, my daughter also decided she was an author—with a book to finish. I acknowledge the brilliance of children, of my children, in their humble pursuit to be like their father. In so doing, they taught me much and made the evenings and weekends of writing take on a stronger purpose. My children have asked when the book would be done so we would have more time to play, but have never made me feel guilty or that I was letting them down. It would not be an acknowledgment section without first acknowledging and thanking my family. My wife is now elevated into sainthood (she has the last name for it) for her tireless devotion and making sure things ran smoothly around the house.

This was a book that has been inside my head for a few years—and through the tireless devotion of friends and family, it has finally taken shape, been distilled, and is available. The starting point was a meeting in Denver with Dave Avrin, a friend for life. Had he not suggested I get started, the book may well still be in my head. I also need to thank Barbara Munson, the editor who challenged me to write a better book.

The process of writing a book, for me, has been a journey. Turns out that, while speaking comes naturally to me, writing required learning and a lot of practice! This journey was sometimes emotional, sometimes intellectual, but always valuable. Early in the process, I sent out a call for help—to validate the concepts and approach. The response was overwhelming and helpful.

I am eternally grateful to Dean Robert Constable—his candor and support taught me much and contributed greatly to the final book. I see now how less is more. I look forward to many more enlightening discussions and growth.

At risk of overlooking those who validated concepts, helped me focus and distilled key points, listened to me and reviewed numerous drafts in various states, I would like to thank: Michael Santarcangelo (the original), Bob Hagen, Todd Colvin, Scott Angelo, Clinton Campbell, Kathleen Santarcangelo, Rick Spratt, Jim Lippard, Ioana Justus, David Mortman, James Costello, Lisa Costello, Adam Dodge, Kevin Baird, Jason Santarcangelo, Todd Bergstrom, Scott Barlow, Clint Kaiser, Jason Appel, Matthew Steele, Sean Forrester, Bill Feth, Cari Endicott, Mike Miller, Adam Bixler, Ron Woerner, John Sileo, Sue Baumes, Charles Boling, David Stelzl, Marty Manjak, Jeff Ewing, Andy Willingham, Scott Wright, Craig Nelson, and Patrick Romero.

Contents

Introduction

"To accomplish almost anything worthwhile, it is necessary to compromise between the ideal and the practical."
—*Franklin D. Roosevelt*[1]

- In 2005, CardSystems Solutions, a billion-dollar credit card processing company, suffered a breach so catastrophic it was sold in a fire sale for 5 percent of its one-time value. For failing to protect the information entrusted to it, CardSystems met with a speedy demise.[2]

- The current and former operators of Los Alamos National Laboratory, having failed to protect classified data that was compromised in a security breach, were fined $3.3 million in 2007 by the U.S. Department of Energy. The enforcement actions followed months of investigation into the breach, in which a contract worker at Los Alamos downloaded classified nuclear data onto three USB thumb drives, which were found in a trailer owned by the worker.[3]

- Data broker ChoicePoint Inc. agreed in 2007 to pay a $10 million federal fine over security breaches that exposed more than one hundred and sixty thousand people to possible identity theft. "Privacy experts" praised the settlement as a warning to companies to get more serious about protecting sensitive information.[4]

Data breaches know no boundaries. In the United States, more than eighty-six percent of companies have detected and responded to at least one actionable breach. Sixty-one percent of companies reported having six or more breaches in a year.[5]

In 2007, 62 million records were compromised here and overseas.[6] Recent focus on breaches has produced a myriad of research reports and analysis, helping to cast light on this growing epidemic. Unfortunately, the real culprit, as we shall see, has been misidentified.

Information is the lifeblood of the modern organization, yet money and resources are being wasted every day in the name of "information protection" and are failing to produce results. Data protection and disclosure laws focus on the notion of disclosure, yet fail to actually protect information. We have limited our concerns to *electronic* breaches caused by outsiders, yet the most common breaches occur internally—and to overlooked, unprotected sources.

The truth is we are focusing on the wrong problem: a breach is only a symptom. Paradoxically, we face a human problem *where people are not the problem.* The problem is that people have been unintentionally—but systematically—disconnected from the consequences of their decisions. As a direct result, they do not take responsibility and are not held accountable. Treating a breach as the problem only makes this worse. For decision makers, instead of simply throwing more technology at the problem, as has traditionally been the case, the challenge of protecting information—in all forms—requires a shift in thinking and a change in behavior within our organizations. This is not bad news. Organizations stand to win big by following a strategy that both protects information and builds thriving organizations.

★ ★ ★

As a security consultant for a number of major businesses in the United States, I have seen firsthand how organizations are struggling with this expensive issue of protecting information and shifting the behavior of users. Organizations continue to throw money into a technology answer to treat the symptom.

After all, they reason, breaches by their very nature involve technological systems that fail—and are caused by outsiders, as in the cases of CardSystems and Los Alamos, right?

Not exactly . . .

MYTH #1: OUTSIDERS POSE THE BIGGEST THREAT TO INFORMATION

Consider this: 70 percent of breaches are actually caused by employees.[7] Instead of an external, nameless threat attacking the network, the source of a breach is more likely to be a well-intentioned employee—a parent, a community volunteer, a model citizen.

Here's a common scene that plays out in organizations across the country: it is 4:45 on a Thursday afternoon and soccer dad has already shifted focus to the game that is about to start; the game for which he will be late. As he juggles deadlines and looks at the work piling up on his desk and in his e-mail, he faces the struggle of meeting both needs in the best way he knows how. He decides to bring his work home with him. He grabs his trusty USB drive and downloads the information he needs for later. Because he is not entirely sure which documents he might need—and wants to make sure he can get his work done—he decides to "play it safe" and copy as much information as he can fit on the USB device.

At the game, he reaches into his pocket to get a piece of gum, and after fumbling around with the contents, he pulls the pack from his jacket. In all the commotion of the play on the field, he does not realize that the USB drive has now fallen to the ground. He continues cheering and heads home when the game is over. It is only much later in the evening that he realizes the drive is missing. Potential for a breach? You bet.

But wait—what if he had managed to arrive home with the drive? The data may still be at risk. Most workers will use the family computer. Focused on working to meet the deadline, he copies the information from the USB drive—all of it—to the home computer. Because this computer is connected to the Internet and shared by the family, it is now subject to another round of risks. In a worst-case scenario, the information ends up on the Internet, causing a massive breach.

Situations like this happen every day. Well-intentioned employees make thousands of good decisions, but it only takes one bad decision to lead to a disastrous breach. Claiming this is isolated or not likely to happen is naive. Average workers will consciously ignore policies that they do not understand or they believe impede their ability to get their jobs done. In a recent "confessions" survey conducted by RSA, The Security Division of EMC, 86 percent of respondents are aware of corporate security policies, 35 percent admit to circumventing those policies, but 65 percent routinely— and knowingly—carry sensitive information on laptops, USB drives, and other portable devices, and 8 percent admit to having lost that information.[8] As we will see, the average employee *is* well-intentioned, but poorly tooled and supported by the company.

MYTH #2: INFORMATION PROTECTION NEEDS A TECHNOLOGY SOLUTION

The reaction to a breach is often an understandable cry for more and better technology. This is an expensive fix—and not really a fix at all. Recently, while working in my capacity as a consultant with a company that had experienced a breach, I learned they spent half a million dollars *in a weekend* because an employee took an action designed to make his job easier. It put the company at huge risk.

This book came about after I came to see that we are facing a human issue here, not a technology one. Using my formal training from Cornell University as a social scientist, I continued to work with clients "in the trenches" to apply ideas from economics, sociology, psychology, education—with some common sense mixed in—to distill to the real problem.

I have learned three things:

1. A breach is a symptom, not a problem.

2. Technology is not the sole problem or answer.

3. The solution lies within the human element.

I do not mean to overstate the cause of the human element and minimize the role technology plays. Actually, the emphasis placed on the human element is two-fold:

1. Human factors have been ignored and downplayed for so long that they must now be considered and addressed in a way that feels new. With this new focus, it may appear that people are the whole solution. Although people play the key role, success comes from blending people and technology.

2. Moreover, to be successful, technology and the resulting controls on technology must be considered, selected, and deployed to *serve people*, which is a departure from the predominant efforts of today.

MYTH #3: PROTECTING INFORMATION COSTS TOO MUCH

By restoring personal responsibility—an attribute of successful companies that has almost disappeared from today's organizations—and adopting the new Strategy to Protect Information contained in this book, every organization stands to benefit significantly. In effect, they will be able to take advantage of more revenue opportunities and bolster their bottom lines by managing people, information, and risk more efficiently.

Taking the bold steps outlined here to engage people can lead to far more than just secure information. Why? It is simple, really:

When people are engaged and feel a part of the organization, they are more thoughtful and caring about being a part of the company and achieving its goals.

★ ★ ★

The Strategy to Protect Information revealed in this book is not "new," groundbreaking, or earth shattering. Let me quickly say that you will not need to purchase expensive technology or spend untold hours to implement it. It is a plan that is based on common sense and can work within any organization.

The strategy contained here consists of three parts:

1. Understand the information of the organization.

2. Engage, empower, and enable people.

3. Optimize solutions.

Into the Breach is for executives and other decision makers who need to demonstrate real results in managing people, information, and risk. The principles explained here can be applied to businesses large and small. It works for nonprofits, state agencies, education—lower and higher—and even businesses with one to three employees.

The Strategy to Protect Information is a five-phase program that can be implemented in 13 weeks or less. By improving information and communication in a semi-structured manner, individuals and organizations manage risk more effectively. The fact that this is a *strategy* is important. It is not another template to be hammered into place in a one-size-fits-all approach. Nor is it a list of useless platitudes. It is a *plan of action that gets results.*

This is a book to be read, absorbed, and acted on. How the strategy is tailored is left to you. As you turn the page and begin your journey, mark the chapters, test the concepts, and take this innovative strategy and make it your own. In fact, experiencing the shift in thinking and seeing the changes in behaviors takes only 15 minutes a day for a few weeks—no radical, expensive changes or sweeping new initiatives.

Part One of this book explains the human factors at play. By exploring the elements that unintentionally led to the current state of affairs—and reliance on popular, but ineffective solutions—you gain the insights necessary to influence the change in a way that is easily received. Understanding people in the context of protecting information is combined with a different perspective on managing risk—setting the stage really to dive into the Strategy to Protect Information.

Part Two lays out the Strategy to Protect Information and its implementation plan. In addition, the core elements of a successful pilot program are outlined, capped off with a discussion of how to budget and invest in a program of this nature.

Part Three shares some considerations for extending and enhancing the strategy to address common issues—including metrics, compliance, and outsourcing.

Part One

1 | Breach: A Human Problem

"What is popular isn't always right. What is right isn't always popular."

—Unknown

In November of 2006, Starbucks reported that four "retired" laptops were missing.[9] Two of them contained data on more than sixty thousand employees—including their names, addresses, and social security numbers. In a twist of fate, the employee(s) who mishandled the laptops were probably also affected by the organization's failure to protect the sensitive information the laptops contained. Had the individual(s) taken responsibility for the information entrusted to their care and considered the consequences of their actions beforehand, the outcome would have been very different.

Despite the cries that breakdowns in security are problems of technology, the statistics say otherwise. People—not technology—cause more than 70 percent of reported breaches. Of this number, 40 percent of incidents are the result of laptop loss/theft and 30 percent are caused by the poor decisions of individuals. *Educational Security Incidents'* "2007 Year in Review" reported that employee actions (unauthorized release of information and equipment/info loss) outnumber "hackers" as the cause of a breach 2:1.[10]

Ironically, these statistics are sometimes used to defend the notion that people *might be* the problem, but the solution still lies in better technology. Technology, the argument goes, can counter the actions of people. This rationale misses the big picture.

The problem and the solution are the people. Period. People at work are disconnected from the consequences of their actions, leading to a situation where they fail to take responsibility and their employers are challenged to enforce accountability. *This* results in an employee "misplacing" four laptops with sensitive information.

Breach is a human problem and the real solution requires restoring responsibility in a way that allows individuals to exercise better judgment. Technology can aid them in this endeavor but will never replace them.

TECHNOLOGY MASKS THE PROBLEM

As the media works to capture attention, sell newspapers, and grab ratings, it influences perception of a growing problem and perpetuates a convenient scapegoat—in this case, the media has focused on technology. The unintended by-product is the conclusion, however shortsighted, that as a technology problem, information protection must require a technology solution. The members of the media are not intentionally misleading but have themselves been misled and have been focusing on the symptoms of breach instead of on the cause.

Here is why: when it comes to the reporter's task of getting explanations on highly specialized issues—like information security—he or she will seek out "experts" for insight. Because the early reported breaches were said to come as a result of database and other technology-related mishaps, the natural action for the media, when covering a "computer security breach," has been to seek out a "computer security expert." Most experts are highly technical, and when asked the question "Why did this happen?" the answer is almost always technical in nature.

"If it bleeds, it leads" is a common quip about the media. When it comes to breaches, sensational stories grab more attention than mundane mistakes. Let's face it—a story about a soccer dad leaving work and dropping his USB stick at a soccer game is boring news. Exciting news is reporting a story about lone "hackers" donned in the appropriate Goth garb, working late into the night to carry out their attacks—complete with black lights and smoke machines.

Goth invaders aside, if we blame technology we are masking the real problem—the human element. And, a breach is only a symptom of a larger challenge in managing people, information, and risk. By continuing to view a breach as a problem of technology, we also continue the long-perpetuated belief that individuals are not to be held accountable. This further reduces personal responsibility at work. Without people taking responsibility, the problem is then projected back onto technology, and a technology solution is sought. This is a dangerous cycle.

The approach of throwing technology at the problem of breach simply is not working.

SUPPORT PEOPLE THROUGH TECHNOLOGY

Success comes when the human factors at the core of this challenge are addressed in a way that engages people and supports them with technology. Thinking that technology alone can solve this problem, like flicking a wall switch to light a room, is tilting at windmills. No automatic switch exists to provide immediate and complete security. True information protection more closely resembles emergency flashlights—you probably know of them. They are operated by a hand crank to generate the power to supply light. Cranking for seconds generates power that is captured and stored to provide light for minutes.

Here is the relevance: the ability to generate this light requires human interaction and involvement—and this is enhanced by technology. The latest emergency flashlights even take advantage of LED and other technology improvements to generate more energy, capture it more efficiently, and provide more light using less power. This makes it easier for the average person to generate the light he or she needs with fewer overall cranks. The emergency flashlight supports people in a natural and intuitive way.

The ability to protect information requires the same marriage of human intervention and technology. The process of protecting information requires a shift in how each person thinks and acts. Just as important, it requires a change in how technology solutions are selected, implemented, and used. The days of selecting a solution and having people conform are over. Now, technology solutions first must be matched to the needs of the individual and designed to make it easier for people to do their jobs while protecting information.

The simpler and clearer the processes to protect information are at recognizing this human element, the more effective people will be at using technology and successfully preventing breaches.

PROTECT ALL INFORMATION

Information is the lifeblood of an organization; it must be protected in all forms and through all uses. We all know this. But the bulk of legislation and regulations governing data focuses narrowly on *electronic data* and *disclosure*. This shortsightedness often overlooks verbal and physical information, as well as changes to the integrity or availability of the information.

Although it is true that massive amounts of electronic information can be moved quickly through electronic means, significant breaches have also occurred via printed material. Let us look at some ways this can occur. In 2006, the *Boston Globe* exposed the bank and credit card information of more than two hundred and forty thousand subscribers when employees used recycled paper—containing discarded internal reports—for nine thousand routing slips used in paper delivery.[11] Employees who accidentally printed reports, and then decided to recycle them, caused this breach when they failed to shred or otherwise dispose of the reports properly. Interestingly, it took a newspaper vendor to alert the *Globe*—none of the employees responsible for printing the routing slips or delivering the newspaper bundles did so.

Or consider how commonplace it is in many organizations for employees to review all of the printed material on or around the printer. In the case of Nassau Community College (NCC), a printout of the entire student body—twenty-one thousand people—was reported stolen when an employee stepped away from her desk for only minutes.[12] As part of the cost of handling this breach, NCC offered one year of credit monitoring to all affected students.

Breaches via printed matter extend to all types of organizations—including professional sports. After the recent "spygate" scandal in which the New England Patriots professional football team was caught illegally videotaping the signals of opposing teams, *NFL Sunday* commentator and former coach Jimmy Johnson explained that, after a game, he and his coaches would routinely search the trash of the other teams to see if they left any valuable information behind. None of us are totally innocent. How many employees throw away drafts of confidential reports in their hotel rooms or in the hotel business center, forget them in the seat-back pockets of airplanes, or inadvertently leave them behind?

Information passed along in conversation can be considered breach material too. Listening to people chatting while sitting in a public space or reception area of a company often yields valuable information that should have been protected. This extends to elevators, conference rooms, hotel lobbies, and more. Modern business's appetite for mobility has led to otherwise confidential calls being held at the Little League game, in the coffee shop, on the train ride home, and in other highly public places. It is worth pondering—do people value privacy or anonymity more? The risk to the organization is the revelation of trade secrets or other sensitive information that can cause substantial harm in the wrong hands.

Taking this one step further, it is also important to ensure the information that companies rely on to make decisions is unchanged and available when needed. Imagine the devastation if a company's database was altered and orders could not be accepted or filled.

Ironically, extreme focus on disclosure of electronic information actually works to disconnect people further from the process of protecting information. The solution to protecting information requires that information in all forms be considered, assessed, and managed. Focusing narrowly on disclosure is the old way. All employees must be prepared to protect the availability and integrity of the information upon which their jobs depend. Ensuring success requires looking at how people do their jobs in a new light.

2 | People Just Want to Do Their Jobs

"Man is by nature good...Men are depraved and perverted by society."

—Rousseau[13]

"SCREAM FOR HELP. SCREAM LOUDLY AND DON'T STOP. I'LL COME find you." This is simple advice that many parents have shared with their children before walking into a mall to prepare them how to act if they get separated. Parents realize the importance of teaching children about the risks of the physical world—and how to protect themselves—in simple and meaningful ways. Generations of experience have been distilled into reminders such as "Don't take candy from strangers." These efforts to protect our children work because the information is shared in a way that allows the child to compare it to his or her own experience and understand the consequences. In other words, the advice is simple, self-proving, easy to understand and remember—and relevant to the child. Children can assess and understand the consequences of their actions in terms of their own experience.

We lack a similar approach to educating employees effectively about the perils of an online world and the associated technological implications. In part, this is complicated by the exciting pace of technology improvement, forcing organizations and individuals to struggle to keep abreast of changes, let alone think about consequences, while trying to do their jobs. Often, the unintended consequences that accompany one's choices are not realized until too late. Take the case of Stacy Snyder, who was removed from a student teaching program and denied her teaching certificate because she posted a picture of herself on MySpace.com in which she appeared to be drinking alcohol. She was above the legal drinking age, but her behavior was "not representative of what was expected." A case is now pending in court.[14]

Many organizations base security policies on the assumption that people *simply know how* to protect information. The reality is that few people have the appreciation for the risks inherent in technology or the experience necessary to exercise good judgment. They lack the "aha moments" that distill experience and guide actions. Unless those insights are captured in a meaningful way that can be distilled and shared with others, people remain left out of the process.

This is not an attack about being technologically illiterate; it's merely meant to shed light on the ongoing challenge of expecting people to make the right decisions and protect information with little or no training, guidance, or practical experience. Comfort with technology does not translate into a heightened ability to protect information. The ability to make effective decisions when protecting information comes from experience. It requires a different approach to connect with individuals in their own words and use their experiences to help them understand the consequences of their actions. *Across generations, we still lack a systematic approach to sharing the dangers with people in actionable ways.* In order to change the approach, the motivation and actions of individuals in the workplace need to be considered in a different light.

THE TWO PRINCIPLES OF PEOPLE AND THEIR JOBS
Given that protecting information is an important challenge for organizations, a challenge that requires participation from

everyone, in most organizations only a handful of people are tasked with the job responsibility of securing information. Most organizations exist based on the successful efforts of employees to get their jobs done. Considering how people do their jobs has led to the realization of two principles:

1. People just want—*and only have time*—to do their jobs.

2. Most people prefer to do the "right thing."

In the decade spanning 1996 to 2006, global worker productivity rose.[15] Although the United States leads the list in terms of gross hours worked and production of wealth per worker at $63,885, nearly every country has seen significant gains. This increase in productivity and hours worked demonstrates that time for activities that are not essential to job performance is limited or non-existent. Still, most employees want to do the right thing and, in most cases, for the right reasons. This presents a challenge, however, if people have never learned the right way to protect information.

Corollary: People can only do the right thing if they know how

Given that few employees are tasked with securing information, most lack the insight, experience, and knowledge to know what the right thing is or how to do it. If they only have time to do their jobs, they are prone to making mistakes because they are not aware of the risks or consequences of their actions.

One of the largest breaches to date occurred when a contractor to the Veterans Administration (VA) brought home a laptop and external drive containing the personal information of 26.5 million veterans and active-duty military personnel. The information was unprotected and subsequently stolen from the contractor's house. In the ensuing investigation, the VA requested $145 million (USD) from Congress to cover credit monitoring for those affected and was threatened with a $45 billion class-action lawsuit—the results of which are still being decided in court. This specific incident ended when the laptop was recovered and forensic review declared the data untouched.[16]

Current efforts directed at protecting information create additional burdens and barriers—real and perceived—just for people to do their jobs. When faced with a choice of getting their jobs done or finding the time to focus on how to protect information—often at the expense of an increasing workload—people naturally choose to focus on getting their jobs done the best they can. At a time when more information is available than ever before, people have less time to process and act on the information. The path of least resistance becomes copying and transporting all of the information, thereby exposing it to risk.

In the context of the two principles—that people just want to do their jobs, and most people prefer to do the right thing—it is understandable, but not excusable, that the contractor for the VA took the information home, without permission and against policy. In fact, although 86 percent of employees admit to being aware of security policies against such actions, fully 35 percent admit to ignoring those policies—simply so they can get their jobs done.[17] People want—and need—to get their jobs done in a way that protects information. It becomes the role of the organization to make it easier for them to do their jobs while protecting information.

Although technology solutions can aid in this process, the sense of individual responsibility that comes from understanding the consequences of action and inaction is core to long-term success. In fact, technology solutions and the standard approach to applying them have deepened the wedge between users and the consequences of their actions.

COMPLIANCE IS NOT A VIDEO GAME

Video games transport a person into a virtual world that has no negative consequences. In business, heavy reliance on technology has created a near-virtual environment that has further disconnected people from the decisions they make. This is evident, for example, in many of the processes and programs that take and publish information on public websites. Health Net Federal Services (HNFS), in what is described as a combination of human and software error, posted the personal information of one hundred and three thousand doctors from 11 states to a public website. Available for more than two months before being discovered, this breach cost HNFS a year of credit monitoring for the doctors involved and may wind up causing the end of the business relationship with some of the organizations.[18]

Protecting information is a process; it is not a video game. *Too many organizations treat security, privacy, and compliance as a video game.* Consequences, whether good or bad, should not be divorced from the actions of the individual.

EXCLUSION: GOOD FOR SELLING, BAD FOR SECURITY

Most organizations today practice security through "exclusion." In Marketing 101 terms, exclusion is a practice that limits or restricts access to create demand. The risk associated with exclusion is alienating or angering potential customers. Exclusion, as practiced in security, occurs when the protection of information is treated only as a technology or policy issue that is the sole responsibility of the security department. In a recent survey, 43 percent of enterprise users declared security to be the responsibility only of IT.[19] This is caused in large part by the systematic practice of exclusion. For years, the IT departments have implemented solutions that only a handful of people understand. Those in the know then reinforce their positions by suggesting that others will not understand, do not need to know, will only cause problems, and cannot be trusted anyway. Exclusion becomes a self-fulfilling prophecy.

The very people who should be accountable and responsible for information have been excluded from the solution.

As a direct result, they pay little care or attention to information under the false belief that "the IT department has it covered." This attitude creates situations where individuals make costly mistakes like these:

- A lawyer for Pepper Hamilton, representing Eli Lily & Co. in a settlement with the U.S. government reaching $1 billion (USD), sent an e-mail in error to a *New York Times* reporter instead of a colleague. Because the lawyer relied on a feature of the technology—assuming it was "covered"—an extensive and highly confidential report became the basis for a front-page story.[20]

- While switching from social security numbers to employee identification numbers—which is a *good* thing—a BJ's Wholesale Club employee lost the USB drive being used to effect the transfer of data. This cost BJ's a year of credit monitoring for the employees affected.[21] They have since updated their policies and provided encrypted drives for future use, but the damage has been done.

These workers most likely had been excluded from the process of protecting information and were told it was "a technology issue." They were not held accountable for their actions. Exclusion prevents people from being aware of the consequences of their actions. Beyond the detachment, it leads to solutions that create pain for users, eliciting what is known as the human response to pain.

THE HUMAN RESPONSE TO PAIN: WHY CURRENT EFFORTS FAIL

Many people erroneously use the words reaction and response interchangeably. A reaction comes without thought or planning; it is a primal action. A response is a conditioned action that is based on planning, practice, and a deliberate methodology to achieve a goal. Reactions to pain are generally quick, clear, and obvious, like when a person jerks a hand away from a hot stove. Responses to pain, however, are more complicated. Many people have been conditioned through sports and other athletic endeavors to believe that "no pain, no gain" and when in pain, find ways simply to push on. When the body senses a duller pain, perhaps an ache, it acts in a more complex manner to address that pain. The body, as a system, *is* remarkable for its adaptability to dealing with pain and essentially distributes the "problem" to more areas of the body, deeper into the core. The organization, it turns out, is no different.

If physical and muscular problems in the human body—often caused by "working through the pain"—are treated in a way that *creates more pain* for the person to endure, the result is the false appearance of progress. The additional pain evokes a natural response of protection that masks and buries the real problem deeper and wider into the body. The result is a more costly and complicated process to actually heal the injury. The same holds true for protecting information.

Security is often practiced in a way that creates pain for the organization by "inflicting" security, privacy, and compliance on people. As people "work through the pain" they have been conditioned to endure, a false conclusion is drawn that the security program is working and information is being protected. Instead, the real problems are being shifted deeper into the organization in a way that is more complex, complicated, and more expensive to correct.

Whether working on the human body or at a human level in the organization, the best and most effective solution is to work within the bounds of comfort, making subtle changes that are able to address the real problem. Sometimes, ancillary problems and challenges have to be addressed before the initial problems can be properly addressed. **Insisting people work through the pain of security evokes the human response to pain and leads to bigger and more complicated problems.**

Here is an example. Most organizations require users to create and use "strong" passwords. The policies are often unclear and confusing, such as this one from Notre Dame:

> Computer users at Notre Dame shall select passwords according to the following:
>
> - Password minimum length: A password must be no fewer than eight characters.
>
>   Though technology constraints may impose maximum length or other restrictions, use of "Pass Phrases" (memorable short sentences instead of single words) shall be supported where possible and practical. The OIT will provide an electronic password management service that will supply timely and detailed information on applicable password limitations.
> - Composition: Passwords must be composed so that they:
>   - include at least one character from at least three of the following classes: lowercase letters, uppercase letters, numerals, punctuation (for example, #, |, $, % and spaces)
>   - are not found in common dictionaries, and are not well-known or predictable phrases (for example, "GoIrish" is a poor choice for a password)
>   - do not resemble the NetID or the name of the account holder
> - Password aging: A Notre Dame computer user must change his or her password at least every 180 days. Attempts to login using an expired password will not succeed. After changing a password, a computer user must

    wait at least one hour before changing his
    or her password again. Expired passwords
    will be accepted as valid only when chang-
    ing one's password, and only by the system(s)
    designated and supported by OIT for this
    purpose.
- Reuse of old passwords: Reuse of any of the
  account's eight prior passwords will not be
  permitted.[22]

Although this is a technically competent policy, identi-
cal to nearly every other password policy I have reviewed, the
jargon and tone of this is certainly confusing. This does little to
help users get their jobs done, threatens them with technology,
and creates a condition of pain they must endure. Organizations then choose technology to enforce these parameters—in
the mistaken belief that forcing compliance technically creates
actual compliance.

Instead, users exercise a *response* to the pain. Users will fig-
ure out how to create a password that is accepted by the system
and then write it down, sometimes on the laptop, keyboard,
or computer monitor. This is easy to check simply by walking around and observing behaviors. People will even freely
share their password. In Britain, 34 percent of people shared
their password freely and, when bribed with a chocolate bar,
more than 70 percent of people shared their password and other
personal information.[23] That must have been an amazing piece
of chocolate.

There are plenty of technology solutions that aim to take
away the burdens of passwords—many of them compelling. The
point here is broader than passwords: when people are inflicted
with a dull pain, they will seek to address it in ways that present the appearance of compliance, while the real problem lurks
below the surface. By failing to address the real problem—in the
case of passwords, teaching people simple strategies and providing

them tools and technology to protect their own passwords properly—the risks and costs associated with repairing those risks increase.

The approach of the organization has a large impact on the response of the individuals. Organizations that take an approach that supports people and actually engages them in the process will reap rewards. An approach many organizations take, however, is one that sometimes appears to get results while exacerbating the very elements of human nature outlined in this chapter—in an approach that resembles a crash diet.

3 | Breaking the Security Diet

"To safeguard one's health at the cost of too strict a diet is a tiresome illness indeed."

—*La Rochefougauld*[24]

EVERY YEAR, AS SWIMSUIT SEASON APPROACHES, MILLIONS OF people prepare their bodies by going on a crash diet. The problem is that dieting this way creates temporary restrictions that are difficult, if not impossible, to sustain. Many dieters give up before reaching their target weight. When a crash diet fails, the resulting frustration causes backlash and blame. Upset at missing their goals while disrupting their schedules, they blame their diets and go back to their former ways, sometimes developing worse habits. The science is clear: sustained weight loss and health are dependent on mindset, lifestyle, and eating habits. This type of dieting, for the most part, fails.

THE SECURITY "CRASH" DIET

As the annual audit—or other trigger event—approaches every year, organizations around the world embark on a security "crash diet" to make sufficient change—or the appearance of change—to satisfy the goal. Company-wide, work is interrupted as people are asked to check boxes on lists, attend required training sessions, and endure changes in the name of security. Once the deadline passes, people return to their old habits, often stressed, angry, and behind schedule. This approach results in no real improvement to security and often creates harm deeper in the organization.

The crash diet helps explain why numerous posters, e-mail campaigns, and other efforts to build "awareness" tend to fail—people continue to leave laptops unattended, leading to their theft. Here are just two examples of how this happens:

- A contractor for the New York City Financial Information Services Agency (FISA) took a laptop containing the details and personal information on more than two hundred and eighty thousand New York City retirees to dinner at a local restaurant. Left unattended during dinner, the laptop was stolen—putting the unencrypted information at risk.[25]
- An employee of Verisign, a company known for providing a variety of security services for Internet commerce, actually had a laptop stolen from his car. It not only contained the personal information of employees but their employment and salary records too. The laptop was only protected by the user password, which can be easily bypassed by thieves.[26]

THE HIGH COST OF FAILED DIETS

Companies have long protected their trade secrets to keep their competitive advantages. As information takes focus as a core organizational asset, the value of that information continues to rise. The rising value of data, as well as the rising costs of handling a breach or other lapse in security, has raised the cost of taking the diet approach to security.

It is helpful to look at the distinction between credit card fraud and identity theft. The former has less overall impact on consumers as the cost burden is shifted to the merchants and vendors. On the other hand, the median loss for victims of identity theft has risen to more than $31,000 per person.[27] This difference in impact is also reflected in the black-market value of such information. Recent reports have put the value of valid credit card information with the verification code at roughly $0.50 to $5 per record.[28] However, information that leads to identity theft is valued differently: each social security number fetches $5 to $7, a complete compromised identity is worth $10 to $150, and bank accounts range from $30 to $400. Because information exists in physical, verbal, and electronic form, it must be considered and safeguarded in all instances, as the opportunity for thieves to profit continues to rise.

This extends to the attractiveness of mobile device theft. Once considered a crime of opportunity, the ever-expanding hard drives designed to contain rapidly growing information are literally rich targets for thieves. An average corporate laptop— probably worth $1,000 or less—has more than $972,000 USD worth of value.[29] In the preceding example, the FISA contractor's laptop held personal information on more than two hundred and eighty thousand people. At the low end of the scale, this has a potential street-value of $2.8 million USD— and that is only for the identities. There is a good chance the contractor had other sensitive and valuable information stored on the same laptop.

The crash diet approach has other consequences to consider: employees taking and sending valuable company information home with them. Consider this: 65 percent of users admit to bringing home sensitive information related to their job on a frequent basis and 63 percent of users also admit to sending work files and information routinely to their personal e-mail accounts (in plain text), in knowing violation of policy.[30] Information of considerable value is leaving the protection of organizations and being kept on home computers and within e-mail systems that are outside of organizational control—like the former contractor for the Department of Veterans Affairs who was found to have 1.8 million records containing personal information on his home computer.[31]

THE NEW FAD DIET: ENCRYPTION

At home, despite the fact that binge diets do not work, people continue to seek out and try new ones. Organizations are no different. Realizing the value of data and rising costs of handling breaches and other security incidents, the fad diet *du jour* is laptop and device encryption. Most fad diets are grounded in good intentions and have some redeeming value but are taken to an extreme at the expense of good health. It is no different with the push for encryption. I believe encryption plays a valuable role in helping to protect information. However, it is a solution that needs to be designed and implemented in a way that supports individuals. Otherwise, it presents a false sense of security—and is no more effective than a fad diet.

Four basic challenges should be addressed when deploying encryption to protect information in the crash diet approach:

1. Encryption systems are complex, double-edged swords and require expert counsel to assess, design, implement, test, use, and monitor. The encryption solution must be implemented in a way that protects information while supporting individuals and organizations. This includes consideration for how the solution will be implemented, how encryption keys will be managed, and how backup solutions will be tested and validated.

2. The standard process organizations rely on is selecting a technology solution and then informing users of the pending change. To users, this is not only perceived as an additional burden to their already compressed schedules but also represents a pain they must endure to complete their jobs. This evokes the human response to pain in which users find clever—but sometimes harmful—solutions to get their job done. A visit to the "help desk" to learn some of the war stories will provide lots of insights.

3. Most organizations practice the exclusion approach, suggesting the solution is technology, and fail to explain the solution in a way that connects with users. Instead, they issue a statement that the problem has been solved. To the user, this means someone else has solved the problem. Now, users are further disconnected from the consequences of their actions, so they tend to engage in some risky behaviors—leaving laptops unattended in public locations, for example—that they would never take with their personal belongings.

4. The real failure of this approach comes after taking a closer look at the real challenges—management of the *key*. Encryption works by having a key that encrypts and decrypts the data. In a misguided effort to ease the burden on users, many encryption solutions rely on passwords. Regardless of whether it requires an additional password or is integrated into the operating system, the assumption is that users will select strong passwords. In theory, this makes sense. In practice, the IT department uses technology to *force* a good password— creating a pain for the user, who responds by writing the password *on* the device. If the password that unlocks the encryption is written on the device, is the information actually protected?

Although encryption is a viable solution, the crash diet approach neglects the necessary shift in thinking and acting that works in conjunction with the technology. The end result is a situation where "security" is assured but not necessarily existent. The bottom line is that organizations cannot afford to ignore human factors. When it comes to encryption, a better approach is to engage users throughout the entire process and work to build a solution that addresses all issues in a way that connects with users' experience and desire to do their jobs while protecting information.

SHIFTING AWAY FROM THE DIET

The current pace of operations for most organizations is hectic and focused on reacting. Systems store, process, and transmit information quickly, setting the expectation that everything must be done on tight timelines. The allure of diets is the claim of immediate results. Without taking time to deliberate and consider different situations, the resulting actions and decisions not only waste money, they put the organization at risk.

This state of reactivity—as witnessed by the increasing number of poorly constructed e-mails, often sent from a mobile device—has created a condition of constant stress. As already explored, people just want to do their jobs, and they want to do them right. The culture of speed, combined with a hyper-focus on technology, has disconnected people from the process. During times of high stress, employees lack the capacity to absorb new information and process decisions effectively, and they end up making mistakes. Their course of action may be deemed less risky to their job but not always less risky to information. This constant stress actually works to disconnect people from their decisions, furthering the chance that they will make a mistake with disastrous consequences. To change the way people protect information, the mindset needs to be shifted and the love affair with the "security diet" needs to be ended.

The challenge comes in changing what is broken but still works. This is not a change that can be made through policy alone. The necessary shift in thinking that drives a change in behavior can be incremental but requires effective leadership and a restoration of power to the individual.

LEAD WITHOUT BEING LOUD

People do not need to be told what to do. They need to be shown. Leadership is about action and the ability to influence—the real power of a leader is not often expressed in words or even action but in results.

To lead this change and ensure information protection organization-wide, it is important first to understand the experience of the individual. This often requires active dialogue and careful listening—not only to what is said but to what is *not* said. This is a fine point: instead of focusing on protecting information, a leader makes it easier for others to do their jobs *and* protect information.

Efforts can be evaluated with a simple question: "Is this going to make it easier for people to do their jobs?" If the answer is anything other than yes, then it needs to be carefully considered. Making an individual's job harder only leads to pain and the complications and increased costs that follow. Engaged leaders, in touch with all elements of an organization from the ground up, have a more complete perspective and overall more accurate understanding of process, information, and how that information is being used.

By adopting a path that makes it easier for people to do their jobs—and supports them in the process—less money and resources are wasted solving larger problems that could have been avoided. This allows the opportunity to step back while considering the needs of individuals in conjunction with the needs of the organization. This improves all aspects of an organization and leads to increased revenue, decreased costs, and the effective management of people, information, and risk.

PUSH POWER TO THE INDIVIDUAL

What people do when no one else is watching ultimately decides when and how technology is going to be used and information protected. Although advances in technology will continue to aid and guide decisions, people have to participate in the process to be able to make better decisions. In shifting power to the individual, the goal is not to create an army of security experts. People have jobs to do; engaging them in the process allows them to understand the consequences of their actions in the context of their jobs—in their words, based on their experiences. This allows people to become truly aware in the simplest terms. This awareness will allow them to be proactive and exercise judgment to the best of their ability.

Extending power to individuals and engaging them in the process not only benefits them but also provides an important window into the foundation of the organization. Restoring accountability and responsibility and inviting people to partici-pate in the process allows them the opportunity to make real contributions to the company and have a direct outlet to share their ideas, passions, and knowledge. This provides confidence that the right decisions will be made, and works to inform the process of risk management, crucial to the ability of an organiza-tion to manage people, information, and risk.

4 | The Solution: Manage People, Information, and Risk

"The best way to solve any problem is to remove its cause."
—*Martin Luther King, Jr.*[32]

SEVEN YEARS OF WORK—GONE IN SECONDS. WHEN A WOMAN IN Tampa read a help-wanted ad for what appeared to be her job, she concluded she was about to be fired and decided to extract revenge. She walked into the office on a weekend and deleted everything from the server of the architectural firm where she worked, causing about $2.5 million (USD) in losses. Actually, her job was never in jeopardy; it was her boss advertising a position for his wife's company.[33] No one ever expects a breach or attack causing the loss of personal or business information to happen until it's too late.

The nature of security combined with the media coverage of the breach epidemic makes it somehow easy to believe that because nothing bad *has* happened, nothing bad *will* happen. This perspective creates a challenge for effective risk management. With 85 percent of businesses reporting a loss of data in the last two years, and 81 percent of businesses compelled to notify customers of that loss, it is more likely that something will happen.[34] The latest cost of handling a breach is $197 per record. The continued failure to protect information, coupled with rising costs of handling those breaches, requires attention. Rather than simply applying technology, the solution lies in understanding and managing the risk—and in managing people, information, and risk in an approach that builds a culture of risk management.

THE RISK MANAGEMENT CONTINUUM

Risk management is the art and science of assessing risk and taking actions to accept, reduce, or transfer risk to tolerable levels. Successful risk management requires accurate understanding of the information, threats, and actions of the organization. The security risk to an organization is often expressed on a continuum, ranging from too little security on the left to too much security on the right. The presumption follows that somewhere in the middle lies a magical line of "just right."

The consequences of too little security result in conditions that lead to breaches and other failures to protect information. At the other extreme, too much security not only wastes money but creates unnecessary burdens on individuals, evoking the human response to pain. To avoid wasting money, information and systems have to be prioritized and addressed based on those priorities.

However, this linear approach to assessing security is not effective and should be reconsidered. Not ensuring information and systems are understood and prioritized leads to a more common situation of having too much *and* too little security at the same time. This combination is dangerous, because key areas may be left unprotected while other areas are over-protected, presenting the appearance of good risk management. These situations are problematic because they are false security or "Security Theater"—looks good, but beyond entertainment, provide little value and create situations that increase, not decrease, risk.

EFFECTIVE RISK MANAGEMENT

Beyond simply managing risk, the way to avoid or reduce the costs of a lapse in security is to establish and practice *effective* risk management. The distinction of effective risk management is an emphasis on prioritizing and acting on complete and accurate information. With a more informed picture of information—including how it is used, stored, and protected by individuals—organizations are more likely to develop a realistic and actionable understanding of the true risk factors. With better information comes the opportunity for better decisions.

In order to make the right decision to accept, reduce, or transfer risk, confidence must exist in the process. *Note: ignoring or being ignorant of the risk is tacit acceptance.* This requires a defined process that is exercised and evaluated in the context of the specific risk tolerance and an accurate depiction of the specific risk, including the probability of realization, frequency of occurrence, and the potential impact to operations and resources. In the event of a breach or other lapse in security, the actual impact can be measured against the expectations to inform and improve the process. Ironically, 29 percent of businesses that suffered a loss of information failed to calculate the financial impact, with 11 percent flatly explaining they did not want to know![35]

The tolerance levels are formed by the business. When I was a young consultant on a global banking project, my team was tasked with assessing the risk to an application before it was released to consumers. Our team concluded the risk to carry $1 million of impact. We presented our finding to the risk committee with the recommendation that implementation be delayed until a solution could be put in place to reduce what we believed to be an unacceptable level of risk. After carefully listening to our assessment, the business decided it was going to put the program in production anyway. Dismayed, my team protested. Only then did I understand the power of risk tolerance and the need for the business to set the tolerance: the application was projected to earn ten times our estimate of risk—in the first 90 days. The risk we demonstrated was truly acceptable to the organization. In the end, everyone agreed to continue to explore ways to reduce the risk while the business released this important application and I learned an important lesson about risk tolerance.

BARRIERS TO EFFECTIVE RISK MANAGEMENT

A common challenge in risk management is moving past the notion that because nothing has happened, or more properly, has been detected, no problem exists and any further effort is a waste of time and money. This seems a lot like the disclaimers of investment companies: *past performance does not guarantee future success; investments pose some risk to principal invested and may result in loss.* Just because you have not experienced a lapse in security—or been able to detect it—does not mean that it will never happen. However, lacking that fundamental "experience" of having lived through a lapse, it is often difficult to be successful. Compounding the challenge are three barriers to effective risk management:

1. Perception

2. Scale

3. Probability

1. Perception

"Perception is reality" is a common marketing axiom. As this axiom suggests, understanding of information, people, and risk is shaped by the perception of a variety of factors. Understanding the impact of perception improves the effectiveness of risk management. When learning that people are the leading cause of breach, many perceive that people must be the problem. Yet this book explains why people are not the problem.

Let's explore how language, context, and experience influence the perception of risk through the demonstration of a logic puzzle devised by Peter Wason in 1966.[36] In the basic approach, four double-sided cards are presented. Each card has a color on one side and a number on the other:

THREE | EIGHT | BROWN | RED

Decide which cards to turn over in order to prove the statement: "A card that displays an even number on one side must also display a primary color on the reverse."

This is an abstract problem to solve. Lacking the language and experience to understand the choices rapidly, this "selection task" results in an abnormally high percentage of failure—by selecting the wrong card. In risk management, this is the same as asking people about risk factors using a language or jargon they do not fully understand based on experiences they may not have. Many who manage security risk have had "aha moments" that have crystallized their experiences, and spend countless hours working through and learning the language and elements to allow them to be more successful.

When the language and context is shifted to a social context in which people are more familiar, the success rate is nearly reversed from the initial failure rate. Consider again the four double-sided cards—still with a number on one side but now with a picture or word on the other side:

FIFTEEN | TWENTY-THREE | BICYCLE | CAR

Now decide which cards need to be turned to test the rule: "Only people over the age of 16 can drive cars." Most people are able to make the right selection quickly. Even individuals that managed to work through the logic of the first puzzle to make the right selection find an easier time with this second task.

This demonstrates the importance of using familiar words and context when assessing risk to get accurate results. In practice, the focus is on addressing specific risk factors using the power of perception, instead of asking people about their perception; by removing perception as a barrier, individuals are able to contribute to the overall success of the risk management program. *The key to managing risk effectively is ensuring the risks are perceived properly and the consequences explained in a language that can be easily understood.*

2. Scale

The human brain is not wired to understand large and complex numbers.[37] We are naturally able to handle simple numbers that guide more instinctive tasks. It is easier to size up a crowd of five people than to estimate how many people are in an entire state. This does not mean that people are incapable of understanding the numbers; it means that we do not instantly understand and act on elements that are out of scale without additional effort and consideration. Test this by imagining a one-inch stack of newly minted U.S. dollar bills. How many bills are in that stack? (Answer to follow.)

The same forces are at work when a consumer learns of a breach that compromised millions of accounts. To the average person, a "significant" amount—a completely subjective measure—is the cost of buying a car every few years. Cars are measured in tens of thousands of dollars. When a breach is reported with hundreds of thousands or even millions, the number is too large to comprehend and either seems alarming or is too big to cause concern; scale works in the favor of the organization that suffered the breach. Numbers this big are out of the realm of general understanding. As a result, it becomes as meaningless as telling a four-year-old her birthday is nine months away. When asking people how many bills are in a one-inch stack, guesses range from 50 to 500—because people are working to assess the answer in the scale of the dollar amount. For the record, there are 233 newly minted bills in a one-inch stack.[38]

Advertising effectively uses scale. A successful ad campaign explains four out of five dentists recommend their gum. This is easy to visualize and understand. Imagine if they tried to explain 80% of thousands of dentists recommended them—it would be confusing and lose the impact. Instead of advertising their weekly costs, business newspapers appeal to readers to subscribe "for less than a cup of coffee." By changing the scale and equating it to a popular good—coffee—consumers quickly relate.

When assessing and managing risk, the same factors apply: the larger and more out of context the numbers, the harder it will be to gain an accurate understanding. By reducing or changing the scale to a more natural element, information that would otherwise be ignored can be easily understood, absorbed, and acted on. Using pictures or other visual representations enhances this process by drawing people in and allowing them a richer experience. Explaining to someone that the earth is 5 billion years old and that human existence is estimated at 200,000 thousand years are both numbers too large to understand rapidly. However, when a 400-sheet (roughly standard) roll of toilet paper is unrolled down a long hallway and used to represent the entire history of the earth, different elements can be visually plotted.[39] At the end of the roll, human existence would take up a small slice of that final sheet, a space roughly two to three fingers in width. Viewing the unrolled timeline brings the scale of billions of years relative to human existence rapidly into focus.

3. Probability

Assessing the probability—the likelihood—of an event is a challenge for protecting information because success is usually measured by what is not seen and does not happen. Often considered the realm of technology and technologists, probability poses a unique challenge: many believe, loudly, that if they can exploit a vulnerability to a system then anyone can. Although the threat of attack is real, the probability of it actually being realized has to be questioned. Most people have no idea how to exploit a vulnerability, let alone how to influence the mix of conditions required to execute it successfully. This perception that outside attackers exploiting vulnerabilities represent the largest threat has skewed the ability of organizations to get the probability right. In recent reports, penetration from outsiders has fallen to the third most likely cause of breach, with only 22 percent of breaches. Unauthorized disclosure is the top at 38 percent and theft comes in at 28 percent, comprising two-thirds of reported breaches.[40]

By leveraging the power of perception and impact of scale, the entire user base (or selected samples) can be engaged in the process and asked about risk in a way that harnesses the collective experience, improving the overall measure of probability. It does, however, come with a trade-off: probability rankings are assigned a likelihood of high, medium, or low—a simplified measure of scale that leads to a less precise overall measure. However, a less precise but more accurate measure that helps to build a culture of risk awareness outweighs more accurate probability estimates in most organizations.

As the challenges of managing people, information, and risk continue to be studied, new reports and research are being made available. These efforts reveal more information about the true nature of the threat—with updated information on the probability. This allows the risk management process to be informed by independent research collected over thousands of organizations, as opposed to the good intentions of a handful of individuals who may have let their biases color the results (unintentionally).

THE EFFICIENT FRONTIER OF RISK MANAGEMENT

The efficient frontier of risk, introduced in the 1950s, transformed the way financial managers consider their investments in an effort to get the best results with the least amount of risk.[41] This research demonstrated that when all information was known, a curve that demonstrates the most efficient combination to get results at a specific risk tolerance could be plotted. As with other elements of life, taking on more risk leads to higher reward. Building on these same concepts, managing risk to people and information can be handled efficiently when an accurate—and complete—understanding of information, systems, potential risks, and outcomes is combined with the organization's tolerance for risk. This information can then be used to experience the lowest risk for a given level of return.

Although it may not be feasible or even possible to have the absolute level of detail to reach a true efficient frontier, considering the elements and striving for efficiency leads to an overall improved handling of risk. In practice, this can be examined in the context of the common risk assessment. At the conclusion of the assessment, the findings of risk are often presented in a matrix with severity of risk represented with a color: red for high risk demanding immediate action, yellow for medium risk, and green for low or acceptable risk. Most people assume that the more green in a risk assessment, the "better" the risk assessment with lower overall risk. As a measure of evaluation, risk managers and business leaders push to have as many areas shaded green as possible. Is this efficient—is green really good?

The challenge is to understand the efficiency of the organization relative to the tolerance of risk, based on the known outcomes. Given the oft-changing nature of threats and the shifting importance of information, here are two reasons why green is not good:

1. Areas reported as "green" are often misinterpreted as being complete and requiring no further attention. The problem with this approach is that risk assessments are static "snapshots in time" of a dynamic environment. Elements considered complete based on the snapshot are often ignored in favor of other tasks and solutions—only to become a larger risk.

2. An assessment that results in "green" results may actually indicate that relative to the risk (and risk tolerance) money and resources that could have advanced the organization have been wasted.

When considering risk management on the efficient frontier—where all elements are known, monitored, and evaluated according to risk tolerance—high risks marked as "red" need to be addressed. However, real progress comes by effectively and actively managing risks that are in the shades of yellow, as they provide the maximum organizational benefit with the lowest overall risk. In a dynamic environment, this means risks are regularly being evaluated and addressed in the most efficient way.

Although reaching a true level of efficiency is less likely, applying the concepts of efficiency will improve overall effectiveness. The Strategy to Protect Information outlined in the second part of the book introduces a simple method to engage individuals in the process of managing risk. By increasing individual participation and incorporating technology that enables better decisions, the overall mindset of the organization shifts to one that more accurately identifies and addresses risk. By taking an approach that improves not only communication but the understanding of risk through an improved management of people, information, and technology, the organization improves. The easiest path to success is to adopt a strategy—a plan of action that informs a mindset—throughout the entire organization.

Part Two

5 | The Strategy to Protect Information

"Strategy is the art of making use of time and space. I am less chary of the latter than the former. Space we can recover, lost time never."

—*Napoleon*[42]

CHANGING THE WAY PEOPLE PROTECT INFORMATION IS A complex and dynamic challenge that requires a simple and direct approach. The Strategy to Protect Information, as outlined in this book, is distilled from more than a decade of success in helping people and organizations protect information. Instead of focusing on complex solutions that increase costs, the strategy engages people in the process of protecting information while guiding efforts to those that bring the best reward. Rather than wasting time and money building a complicated solution to pick fruit at the top of a tree, the strategy focuses first on the low-hanging and already ripe fruit before driving the need for more advanced solutions.

The simplicity of this process does not force a new approach. The Strategy can be applied to any organization or against any challenge easily. It can be incorporated into existing programs to enhance their effects, including in highly regulated industries that may have little opportunity to select alternate models.

The Strategy to Protect Information and manage risk has three steps:

1. Understand the information and information resources of the organization.

2. Engage, empower, and enable people.

3. Optimize process and technology.

STEP 1: UNDERSTAND YOUR INFORMATION AND RESOURCES

The good decisions that organizations depend on are predicated on accurate and complete information. Decisions made about information protection are often done with inaccurate, incomplete, or outright false information—that is, whatever is available or believed to be correct based on misplaced assumptions. The first step in the strategy is to gain a clear and accurate understanding of what and how information is used in the organization. This is more than an exercise in "gathering"; this is a concerted effort to gain the knowledge and insight about how the organization, at the core, operates on the information that is its lifeblood.

Chapter 4 outlined three barriers to effective risk management: perception, scale, and probability. Looking at the bigger picture, those same factors often cloud the true picture of an organization. When striving to assess how information is used, there are a number of key questions to ask:

- What information exists, where does it exist, and in what form?

- Why does it exist? What purpose does this information serve?

- What are the foreseeable future uses?

- Who uses this information, how are they using it, and is it being shared?
- How is this information being stored, transported, and archived?

When seeking to establish a more complete and true understanding of the information landscape, it is important to act in the way of an anthropologist—observe in an effort to learn, without judgment. Direct observation of actions and behaviors yields important insights into how people adapt to get their jobs done, but it may not reveal the entire picture. Judgment and being quick to respond to observed events may actually obscure the ability to gain an understanding. Forming an accurate picture, therefore, requires a combination of observation, asking questions, experience, and common sense. This often necessitates a conscious suspension of judgment paired with an open mind that willingly questions every assumption previously held.

Observation combined with conversation is a powerful approach. In formal methods, this would be considered interviewing; a less formal approach yields similar benefit. A conversation is ultimately more powerful in achieving a deep understanding that will improve the operations of the organization. Keep in mind that when an executive or outsider asks questions about how people do their jobs, the answers given may not be accurate—whether by design or because the answer has not yet been considered. Many people are not currently accustomed to being asked about their jobs without the potential for a negative repercussion. The next chapter outlines a successful approach to gaining this information.

This step often produces results much different than expected—most are shocked to learn where information is kept and how it is used. The explanation is simple: people find a way to get their jobs done, which often means that information is duplicated, copied, transported, and stored in a variety of locations and in situations that are not documented and generally not shared—and may be in violation of policy. The key to effective—and efficient—risk management relies on the ability of decision makers to understand the information and resources of the organization accurately with a grounded and realistic assessment of why and how it is being used.

Seeking to understand how information is used and protected provides two direct benefits:

1. The information that is truly important to the organization becomes more evident; it often is not what is anticipated, but it proves remarkably profound once discovered.

2. Learning how others instinctively protect information often provides a direct solution that can be mimicked by others; encouraging people to adopt and refine natural tendencies is far more effective than attempting to force an unnatural behavior change.

The first step of the strategy is not focused on right or wrong. The mission is simple and the application direct: *suspend judgment and seek to gain as much accurate and first-hand experience as possible to better inform the decision-making process.* Assumptions must be challenged and a true and deep understanding of the information, information resources, and processing trends of the organization need to be understood in new and important ways. Done properly, this step yields incredible value.

The more accurate and complete the information gathered at this stage, the more successful the subsequent steps. This step, which can and should be repeated as often as necessary in the process-driven approach to protecting information, is the single best way to reduce the waste and improve the efficiency of any organization.

STEP 2: ENGAGE, EMPOWER, AND ENABLE PEOPLE
Breach is a human problem that results from the disconnection of people from the consequences of their actions. This has led to

a feeling of a lack of responsibility. In order to restore responsibility, people need to be able to participate in the process of protecting information. They must be engaged, empowered, and enabled—concepts that have been abused but continue to be powerful in their authentic forms. The second step of the Strategy to Protect Information brings about purposeful and constructive participation of people to take an important role in the protection of information.

This step focuses on the ability to improve understanding through dialogue, which often increases the natural tendency to protect information as people gain the insight to consider their actions. Although this step will improve overall decision-making—key to reducing risk and improving efficiency—the goal is not to create an army of security experts. Much as an athletic coach reminds his team that their performance is dictated by how they practice when he is not looking—employees who make better decisions when no one is looking improve the overall organization.

As people are engaged, empowered, and enabled, the organization must move to support them with the appropriate information, tools, and support they need to be able to contribute. There are two key elements to making this successful:

1. Leadership must be committed to the conversation.

2. Support must be extended with appropriate tools and other resources to enhance contribution.

Engagement starts with permission

Engagement is measured by attention and participation. Although it may seem like a page from Management 101, the fact that people have been disconnected for so long means they need to be told they have permission to engage.

No question about it—this is an unusual suggestion in the business world today; people are expected to be engaged from the day they start in their positions. When people are first told they have permission to engage, to challenge, to join the conversation, and to take back responsibility, their actions and emotions are mixed. Some laugh, some act confused, others sense and exhibit a sense of relief. Laughter is good! The important aspect is to free the process to begin, and this is a simple way to do it.

As people participate, often cautiously at first, they will learn from others and by sharing their own experiences. Through this effort, ideas, concepts, and experiences will be suggested, tested, debated, challenged, and improved. The important element of engagement and participation is the opportunity to validate, learn, grow, and build relationships. Relationships, as we know, are crucial to success in life and in business. An engaged workforce is more productive and willing and able to make better decisions.

Empowerment is a dialogue, not a directive

Policy does not empower someone; empowerment is achieved when individuals take action based on an understanding of their decisions and the potential consequences. Empowerment is developed and informed through knowledge, experience, and resources that support and guide decision-making. Empowerment is a process that thrives on active conversation.

When learning through conversation, people apply the information shared against their own experience. Through this process, ideas, terms, and definitions are "negotiated"—a natural way for people to reach agreement on the meaning of key concepts. This does not suggest that terms should be negotiated to have *new* meanings. This is especially true for terms that have well-defined industry standards or industries that are heavily regulated, with dictated terms that cannot be changed. The process of negotiation ensures that everyone shares a common understanding of the language and concepts used across the organization. The result of the conversation is to help people learn to make better decisions—not simply to do as they are told.

Empowerment through conversation and subsequent negotiation happens on a daily basis with colleagues, friends, and family. As I work to guide my children to make good decisions and
learn "right from wrong," they routinely listen to what I have
to say, process the words against their own experience (you can
sometimes see it on their faces), and ask questions in return.
Often, the question will begin with "Is this like the time we ... ?"
Many times, they select a situation that either demonstrates
understanding or is close, and I can work either to explain the
differences or select a different example for them.

Sometimes they lack the experience and we decide to work
together and engage on a "mission" to explore the concept
hands-on, where I actually model the behavior. Through this
process of conversation, we work together to reach a common
understanding that allows my children to be empowered (age
appropriately, of course). What's equally important is that I learn
from every conversation too.

Central to empowerment is effective—and consistent—
communication and trust. Welcoming colleagues into conversation with respect, instead of treating them as an adversary or
burden, goes a long way toward improving this process. Equally
important is cultivating a safe place for colleagues and subordinates
alike to voice opinions, share experiences, challenge information
(rather than the person), and allow them the opportunity to reach
a mutual conclusion they can accept. Once people have an experience with mistrust, it is difficult to engage them in the future.

The easiest way to get started is to ask a question and listen to
the answer. Like listening, active conversation is a skill that requires
the ability to communicate, listen, and find a common ground.
It improves with practice. Regularly engaging in conversations
not only fosters empowerment, it is key to the ability to enable
people. The empowerment dialogue will reveal the understanding of expectations to the user, and the support elements needed
for them to be successful. Those support elements, matched to
the needs of the individual, allow them to be enabled.

Enable people for success

Empowerment provides the authority to act combined with the understanding of how and when to act. Ensuring the right processes, tools, and technology are in place to support those actions enables people. It is impossible to truly enable people without a clear understanding of how they do their jobs. With an understanding of the information landscape, developed in step one, the empowerment conversations provide the insights necessary to enable people to be successful, much like a sculptor chiseling away stone to reveal a masterpiece. Sculpture is about taking away and revealing. Enabling people to protect information better is similar in nature.

The process of enabling is focused on making it easier for the individual to do his or her job. This does not always require a large investment in technology or complete overhaul of the organization. Clearly defined and communicated policies or well-designed processes go a long way toward improving the way people protect information. The implementation process outlined in the next chapter demonstrates how to allocate resources best—and whether focused on policy, process, or technology—to enable people best.

STEP 3: OPTIMIZE PROCESS AND TECHNOLOGY

The third step of the Strategy to Protect Information is a natural extension of empowering and enabling people. The focus is on organizational effectiveness and efficiency through the optimization of processes and technology that makes it easier for people to do their jobs and the organization to get the results it wants. This optimization comes from more accurately understanding how information is used and how people do their jobs.

Key to optimization is a focus on reducing waste and ensuring the right solutions are selected, designed, implemented, and operated in a an efficient way. The single most powerful concept to guide the optimizing process, tools, and technology is matching the solution to the needs of the people—instead of the current, widespread practice of people adapting to the process, tools, and technology.

Continued empowerment conversations provide the raw material and mutual understanding of what needs to be done—with a clear picture of how it needs to be done to get results that benefit the organization. The improved participation stimulated by this strategy improves the frequency and quality of feedback—important lessons learned—during enabling that improves the optimization process.

Although it may be ideal to apply the principles of optimization to new solutions, it is a powerful and useful tool to apply to current ones. This entire strategy can be successfully used to revive stalled projects or even save failing projects. *The focus is on engaging and bringing people into the process of making their own jobs easier.* Conversations that explain in a mutually understood language, built on shared experiences, yield remarkable results. Friction caused by confusion is replaced with cooperation and support—or key information is learned about why an effort should be abandoned.

The more diligently this strategy is practiced, the greater the result. Over time, investments will be more effective and less money will be wasted on solutions that ultimately create more harm to the organization.

6 | Implementing the Strategy to Protect Information

"Plans must be simple and flexible . . . They should be made by the people who are going to execute them."
—George S. Patton, Jr.[43]

THE STRATEGY TO PROTECT INFORMATION IS DISTILLED TO THE three key aspects of changing the way people protect information. The simplicity of the approach is deceptive; the strategy is enhanced through careful implementation that takes advantage of the human factors discussed in the first part of the book. This chapter outlines a five-phase implementation plan that guides the adoption and customization of the strategy to the organization.

This approach, exercised at the team level, improves operations and the way leaders manage people, information, and risk. Managers gain direct insight into how team members use, store, and protect information. The real key to implementing this approach is a lightweight structure that encourages a decentralized approach with standardized central reporting: that is, team leaders have power over when and how to run the program, and their results are captured in an organization-standard way that provides greater overall benefit to capturing information to manage risk effectively.

These five sequential phases can be completed in roughly 90 days by spending only minutes per day:

1. Learn How People Do Their Jobs.

2. Gather and Process Information through Conversation.

3. Prioritize, Benchmark, and Analyze.

4. Build a User- and Information-Centric Plan of Action.

5. Communicate the Program.

The full strategy, much like fine wine, improves over time. However, although wine ages best resting in a cellar, collecting dust, the improvement of these phases comes from practice and engagement. The next chapter shares insights on how to pilot this program and really put the Strategy to Protect Information to work through an initial pilot program and beyond.

PHASE ONE: LEARN HOW PEOPLE DO THEIR JOBS

Effective risk management requires a complete understanding of the information and resources of the organization. Traditional approaches to measure this information rely on external parties, surveys, and checklists—all elements perceived as a burden to endure and which generally result in incomplete, inaccurate, or misleading results. By guiding the thinking of people down a narrow path of disclosure and electronic information only, the *real* information of the organization is often overlooked and unprotected.

The Strategy to Protect Information is designed to engage people and shift thinking. People are asked lightly structured questions about their experiences, successes, and challenges in a language that is comfortable and through familiar contexts. Instead of using electronic surveys and checklists that restrict thinking, nothing is presumed, no lists are provided, and people are allowed to decide for themselves what is important. They then capture and share that information in their own words. This approach works whether teams share the same geographic area or work in remote and virtual settings.

I call this new approach the Individual Information Assessment (IIA). The core of the IIA is five questions—non-technical and free of jargon—printed on one side of a standard sheet of copier paper. The questions are designed to be simple and quick to answer and are crafted along the lines of these:

1. Describe the information or resource that is important to you, including who is responsible for the information. If possible, describe the format (electronic, physical, verbal, or mixed) and whether it is shared with others as a matter of routine.

2. What would be the impact to you as you do your work if this information/resource were . . .

   a. Not available to you when you needed it?

   b. Shared with someone who should not have access, for example, a competitor, client, or the general public?

   c. Tampered with to the point where the information was no longer accurate?

3. How are you protecting this information today?

4. How should this information be better protected?

5. What can the organization do to protect it while making it easier for you to do your job?

This approach has no right or wrong answers—and the IIA is not collected, though it will be needed during the team meeting scheduled for the following week (outlined in Phase Two). To guide the IIA, each participant is provided five sheets of paper and invited to pick the most relevant or essential information or resource to write about—a different element each day—for five days in a row.

Here is why this works:

1. The paper-based approach requires a kinesthetic connection that fosters deeper thought and better overall results.

2. Without being tethered to a computer, participants are free to answer these questions whenever and wherever they want—they have total control.

3. Reading and answering the same simple questions five days in a row—in only five minutes—is enough time to create subtle changes in how people think and act about the information they feel is important.

These questions stimulate thinking in a comfortable way that results in heightened awareness. More importantly, by allowing people to document what information and resources are most important to them, the organization gains invaluable insight into the true nature of people, information, and risk.

PHASE TWO: GATHER AND PROCESS INFORMATION THROUGH CONVERSATION

During the first phase, people are invited to pay attention to the information they find important. However, because the answers to the questions of the IIA are based on their own experience, language, and context, the information needs to be gathered and processed in a way that brings benefit to the individual and the organization. This is best accomplished using a two-step process:

1. Facilitated team/group meeting, lasting approximately 30 minutes

2. Brief individual meeting, generally within a week of the group meeting

The team meeting

The team meeting is how information from the IIA is presented, discussed, and captured in a standard format and language. This is done through a team dialogue that results in a shared understanding of what individuals experience as the key information and resources. By translating individual and team experiences into a company-wide format and language, people will be able to communicate more effectively. Improved communication through a shared language—or a shared understanding of commonly used terms—improves the functioning of the organization by reducing confusion and enhancing the ability to manage people, information, and risk.

After leaving the group meeting, people subconsciously review their answers with the insights they gained discussing their experiences with their team. They literally have a new awareness of their actions and the direct consequences of their actions; perhaps for the first time they realize they are responsible. Recognizing that users may gain new insights during the days immediately following the group setting, the second part of this phase schedules individual conversations with the group leader (manager, supervisor).

Individual discussions

Scheduling a brief individual meeting with each participant brings direct benefits:

- In the conversations, managers are able to validate information and capture new insights, recorded into the same form used during the group meeting.

- In a more private setting, users have greater freedom to express concerns or ask questions they were uncomfortable advancing during the group session.

- Managers have the opportunity to remind all team members directly of their responsibility and learn what actions they can take—or encourage the organization to take—to enable their team more effectively.

This step removes *plausible deniability* of the responsibility of the individual to protect information. The additional benefit of this phase is the integrated training and practice for managers to organize and facilitate group and individual conversations. Encouraging practice of these skills on a regular basis improves the overall ability of the organization to "grow" managers.

PHASE THREE: PRIORITIZE, BENCHMARK, AND ANALYZE

There is no single way to analyze, benchmark, and prioritize information. This step is a flexible and adaptable part of the implementation phase—and each organization should use the good practices they already follow, are required to follow by industry, or deem appropriate. The key elements lie in reviewing the information gathered in the first two phases and ensuring it is accurate and complete. This phase can be completed by the local teams, or handled centrally, perhaps by a dedicated security team. The benefit of having the local teams help—if only with the prioritization—is to gain a deeper understanding of the risk management process. A powerful and easy measure to prioritize information relative to risk is to assess each of the pieces of information gathered by the team in terms of confidentiality, integrity, and availability. This approach is outlined in the U.S. Federal Information Protection Standard 199, and is represented effectively in the table on the next page.[44]

The local team assigns a rating of high, medium, or low—collectively—to each element based on the FIPS guidance. Each element is calculated together to produce a final score. The higher the final score, the more important it becomes to address those elements, subsequent to review and additional analysis. This review may include network or application assessments, as well as additional analysis of critical areas as directed by industry guidance and regulation. With prioritized information, additional analysis ensures attention is paid to those elements that matter most. The goal of this step is to develop a complete and prioritized understanding of the security posture of the organization relative to the prioritized information and resources.

TABLE 1: POTENTIAL IMPACT DEFINITONS FOR SECURITY OBJECTIVES

Security Objective	POTENTIAL IMPACT		
	LOW	MODERATE	HIGH
Confidentiality Preserving authorized restrictions on information access and disclosure, including means for protecting personal privacy and proprietary information. [44 U.S.C., SEC. 3542]	The unauthorized disclosure of information could be expected to have a **limited** adverse effect on organizational operations, organizational assets, or individuals.	The unauthorized disclosure of information could be expected to have a **serious** adverse effect on organizational operations, organizational assets, or individuals.	The unauthorized disclosure of information could be expected to have a **severe or catastrophic** adverse effect on organizational operations, organizational assets, or individuals.
Integrity Guarding against improper information modification or destruction, and includes ensuring information non-repudiation and authenticity. [44 U.S.C., SEC. 3542]	The unauthorized modification or destruction of information could be expected to have a **limited** adverse effect on organizational operations, organizational assets, or individuals.	The unauthorized modification or destruction of information could be expected to have a **serious** adverse effect on organizational operations, organizational assets, or individuals.	The unauthorized modification or destruction of information could be expected to have a **severe or catastrophic** adverse effect on organizational operations, organizational assets, or individuals.
Availability Ensuring timely and reliable access to and use of information. [44 U.S.C., SEC. 3542]	The disruption of access to or use of information or an information system could be expected to have a **limited** adverse effect on organizational operations, organizational assets, or individuals.	The disruption of access to or use of information or an information system could be expected to have a **serious** adverse effect on organizational operations, organizational assets, or individuals.	The disruption of access to or use of information or an information system could be expected to have a **severe or catastrophic** adverse effect on organizational operations, organizational assets, or individuals.

This phase sets the stage to use available budget and resources more effectively. Rather than focusing on perceived needs and exciting new technology, decisions can be made and plans developed based on an understanding of the challenges of the individuals, the trends of the organization, and the needs to gain compliance and reduce risk.

PHASE FOUR: BUILD A USER- AND INFORMATION-CENTRIC PLAN OF ACTION

The results of Phase Three provide a list of prioritized information, systems and any "gaps" that need to be addressed. Easily integrated into a variety of project management disciplines, the fourth phase builds a plan of action that takes both a user- and information-centric approach to improving security. This presents an opportunity to select projects with the greatest benefit to the users and business by protecting key information instead of focusing solely on technology or perceived opportunities.

Several areas are often overlooked that can lead to project failure:

- *Define success.*

    Few projects begin with a clear definition of what success means to this entire project. This definition guides the development of every stage of the project as well as guides decision-making to focus on what is necessary. Although the definition of success may evolve during the life of the project, it is the goal line the entire team is working toward.

- *Focus on making it easier for users to do their jobs.*

    The prevailing question to guide projects and planning is "Will this make it easier for users to do their jobs?" If the answer is no, then the project or approach may need to be reconsidered. This helps focus on solutions that are not only cost-effective in the short run, but that provide long-term benefits that truly protect information. Failing to ask and answer this question is likely to lead to a solution that provides the illusion of security while creating a deeper and more complicated, and therefore more expensive, problem that will need to be addressed down the road.

- *Solutions follow requirements.*

   The most effective way to select the right solution is first to understand the total requirements and distill them into a document to guide the selection. Many organizations have developed a bad habit of selecting a solution before or without defining requirements. It is challenging to implement technology solutions successfully, and even more so without requirements that focus on needs over features. This is where the investment in a professional project manager with the experience to set proper requirements is invaluable. The time spent developing realistic and clear requirements will help in guiding the effective selection of the right technology and tool. Effective requirements are covered in Chapter 12, Successful Outsourcing.

- *Know when to call in outside help.*

   Whether driven by a sense of pride and optimism in the ability of the person and his or her team to get the job done or the fear of asking for budget, some managers struggle with the need to request outside or additional help. The same barriers to effective risk management of perception, probability, and scale present potential snags when trying to make good project management decisions. A common trap for many managers is to hope for the best and just get started without all the facts—which often ends up costing more, not only in terms of budget, but also in terms of timeline and frustration.

   Reaching the right decision is easier when based on fact instead of opinion and feeling. Developing a documented overview of the project—including estimated costs and required skills—that can be reviewed and validated by others helps to ground the effort. As the different elements are documented and verified, it becomes more evident if outside assistance will be needed. Taking the time to build a more complete picture, based on facts and experience, helps to prevent situations where the solution is over-promised but under-delivered.

As these elements are taken into consideration during the entire planning and project management process, the plans will be focused on addressing the priorities of the organization in a manner that serves the people. The final step is to communicate the plans and engage people in the process.

PHASE FIVE: COMMUNICATE THE PROGRAM

Communications courses are required for any educational degree and in any discipline. As time goes by, however, the principles get a bit hazy. They are well worth repeating here. As the pace of business continues to increase, people spend less time crafting messages and sharing information. On the receiving end, people are literally bombarded with information and struggle to sort, prioritize, and understand. Improving communication brings immediate and lasting benefits to the entire organization beyond changing how people protect information. Success requires an understanding of the five principles of effective communication and regular practice:

1. Create

2. Prepare to connect

3. Rehearse

4. Deliver

5. Evaluate and evolve

For information to be meaningful, it must be presented in a way that connects with the receivers—using their language, based on their experience. The key to effective communication is first to create and distill the message before connecting it to the audience for which it is intended. Regardless of the audience, delivery is only 20 percent (or less) of effective communication;

this is where most people tend to invest their time. Immediate gains in effectiveness are realized with a renewed focus on message creation, focus, and preparation.

The more information is considered, distilled, and related to others, the more powerful it becomes. Rehearsing can be literal or can be represented by writing, reviewing, and editing the communication. Regardless of the approach, having it reviewed and working to simplify and distill it is always beneficial. Then it can be delivered through writing, speaking, or whatever method is appropriate.

Much consideration should be given to the most effective way to convey information, as each situation is different. Just as important as delivery is assessing the success of the delivery. Effective communication is not "fire and forget it." Once the message has been delivered, engaging with the audience to learn how they received the message is important. In the event the message did not connect as expected, it can either be explained on the spot or clarified for the mutual benefit of everyone involved.

Although good communication is helpful generally, it is crucial when implementing this program. The user and information plan created in Phase Four needs to be shared in a way that connects with people. Instead of announcing, for example, that a "federated identity management solution" will be employed, which implies that an additional burden is being added to the employee's workload, care has to be given to crafting and delivering a different message. Leverage the words and examples shared during Phase Two—during the team and individual meetings—to show how this new solution will ultimately ease the burden. By explaining how their contributions and insights have improved the company in a way that benefits them—that is, making it easier for them to do their jobs, buy-in is assured.

Taking the time during the project planning elements of Phase Four yields the opportunity to explain the benefits and set realistic expectations concerning the users' necessary involvement. By not keeping them in the dark, the message is conveyed that they truly are the secret to organizational success.

7 | **Putting the Strategy to Work: A Pilot**

"It is easier to behave your way into a new way of thinking than to think your way into a new way of behaving."
—*Kegley's Principle of Change* [45]

SETTING OUT TO RUN A MARATHON IS AN EXCITING CHALLENGE. It must begin with a clear plan that builds up the body to be able to run the distance. Runners know to increase their time and distance by no more than 10 percent each week. The biggest mistake is trying to do too much, too soon. As marathon runners work to build their mileage and their base, they work on their form and ensure efficiency. The key is regular practice.

The Strategy to Protect Information requires the same approach. Each time the strategy is exercised, it will become more powerful and more efficient and produce better results. The more the strategy is used, the more comfortable each step will become. As more people participate, the mindset will naturally shift away from the security diet to one of protecting information.

The best way to get started is to design, implement, and operate a pilot program. This will provide hands-on experience and produce the results necessary to carry the program forward. Consider this:

- A small pilot program of five to ten people can be planned, executed, and evaluated with little investment of time and budget.

- A pilot provides the experience to adapt and improve the approach for an expanded rollout, including training, budgeting, and other considerations.

- By demonstrating early results, the pilot program works to reduce inhibitions to adoption by other segments of the organization.

Because change implies risk, it is important to put the strategy to work in a way that gains immediate and visible results while establishing a foundation for further expansion and success. The power in the strategy comes from engaging people and giving them the power to participate in a semi-structured way, to engage on a timeline of convenience, and to experience the benefits first-hand. Expect that the plan will gain momentum as the process goes forward and is refined.

BUILDING THE PILOT TEAM

The more seasoned and open-minded the pilot team, the more likely the information gathered and changes made to the process will benefit the entire organization. Larger organizations may run a handful of pilot programs to test the strategy in a variety of settings, each yielding important feedback and insights into the large-scale implementation.

There are two basic approaches for selecting the initial pilot team:

1. Pilot with a small, receptive team of five to ten people that already work on the same team or in the same physical location.

2. Pilot with a group of five to ten managers selected from different aspects of the organization.

Option One: Pilot with a small team in a department or location

This option selects a team that already works well together and reports to a leader who is strong and receptive to this approach. When selecting this team, look for two characteristics:

1. A team that will embrace the Strategy to Protect Information and continue to use it.

2. An experienced team with a good grasp of their current jobs and the ability to get involved and participate in a way that will shape the experience for others.

Selecting a strong existing team to pilot this program allows for a quick start, excellent participation, and good results. The positive results allow the program to be easily spread to other teams, especially those affiliated with the pilot team. Demonstrating a success with one team creates excitement and good "buzz" about the program. At the end of this approach, the basic elements will have been tested and modified, and are ready to be expanded.

Option Two: Pilot with a mixed "Team of Champions"

This option requires a bit more planning and may be more complicated to manage because it creates a team of strong and influential managers from key areas of the organization. This team will not only produce results but can form the nucleus of an influential team of champions. A benefit of this approach is the way knowledge, experience, and improved decision-making is spread across more teams during the pilot stage. The resulting success piques more interest and helps speed the natural appetite for adoption. After the initial pilot, many of these champions decide to build on their initial pilot experience and implement the strategy for their own teams.

"Champions," the formal or informal groups of people who see the power and rally to the cause of the Strategy to Protect Information, are vital to the early adoption, success, and continued growth of the program. These influencers will guide the processes and ensure that technology is being selected and used in a way that makes it easier for people to do their jobs. Champions also provide valuable feedback about the process and ways in which the implementation and application of the program can be improved. The larger the organization, the more vital the role champions play. As the strategy spreads, the champions will form the "strong core" that will help shape the norms and procedures for the entire company while ensuring that everyone stays connected to the process.

PLAN FOR SUCCESS

The challenge of the pilot program is to avoid the desire to build a strong team and "wing it." Although it may be possible to get good results with this approach, it does little to prepare the way for other teams. By taking time to plan and document the approach and customize the materials before running the pilot, the organization is able to capture the experience and tailor the strategy. The understanding gained during the pilot phase will allow the pilot team the insight and experience required to modify and fit the materials, training, and approach to the needs of the organization. It is the pilot process that will allow the strategy to be incorporated into the organization.

Depending on the team, it is possible to run the five phases in as little as three weeks. More likely, the pilot program can be planned, executed, and reviewed in 10 to 13 weeks. The longer timeline allows for less interruption and more time to review and process results. Regardless of the timeline, the first two phases produce some exciting—and often eye-opening—results. The balance of the phases builds on those results to move the organization to a more effective state.

CAPTURE AND IMPLEMENT LESSONS LEARNED

At the end of the pilot, it is important to bring the team together to review the process in an effort toward improvement. Focus on what worked—whether it was planned or not—as well as what needs to be changed. When focusing on what went right, seek to understand who deviated from the plan but got good results. Capture what they did and learn how to incorporate it into the plan for others to follow. Depending on the total number of changes, it may make sense to pilot the program again, with another team. Include at least one member of the initial pilot team on the next pilot to help guide the process and educate the members.

The process of implementing a full-fledged information protection program will require regular attention and maintenance. Once the program has been tested enough to move beyond the pilot phase, it will still need to be reviewed. Often, as the program is spread wider and to a more diverse audience, new challenges and opportunities arise. Keep in mind, for the program to work, communication and participation are critical.

EXPAND THE PROGRAM

Once the pilot has proven the program, it must be extended throughout the organization. Traditionally, programs are implemented following a top-down approach—where the leadership announces the program and everyone works to adopt it at the same time. The Strategy to Protect Information lends itself to a different approach, allowing teams to select when and how they want to implement the strategy.

This approach allows managers to be informed about the program and benefits. Once they have been trained in the core elements of the program, they have the power to choose when and how to engage their teams. Based on the human factors explained in the first part of the book, this allows each manager to experience the benefit and take action based on the desire to improve knowledge and operations. By incorporating the human factors and allowing teams control over when and how they engage—within lightly structured parameters—the overall organization enjoys the success.

8 | Measuring Success

"Success can only be measured in terms of distance traveled."
—*Mavis Gallant*[46]

DURING THE 2008 U.S. PRESIDENTIAL RACE, REPUBLICAN candidate Fred Thompson made headlines during a Republican debate when he told the moderator, "I'm not doing hand shows today." The entire field of candidates had just been asked to raise their hands if they agreed with the statement: "Global climate change was a serious threat and caused by human activity." Seemingly unfazed by Mr. Thompson's remark, the moderator replied, "No hand shows today?" Mr. Thompson asked if he would be given an additional minute to respond—to put his answer of yes or no into *context*. When he was denied the request, he explained that he would not participate. When asked by the moderator if his answer was no, he explained that he was not answering without the chance to explain—to the applause of the other panelists and the crowd.

When asked about his comments and actions after the debate, Senator Thompson explained that he was uncomfortable with the debate style approach that reduced every answer to a sound bite, and refused to "further dumb down a monkey process." Many organizations, swept up in the movement to distill reports to numbers that can be displayed in the "dashboard report," end up with the same problem—a "monkey process" that has created a number "dumbed down" to the point of being useless. The current reporting processes need to be challenged on the basis of common sense, and include a method to provide the appropriate context. When the decision maker is disconnected from the context and importance of the number, the resulting decisions may end up creating more problems than they solve.

The goal of risk management is to make effective decisions based on available information; the goal of measurement is to evaluate the effectiveness of those risk management decisions. Shifting the way people think and protect information requires a shift in the way success is measured. Despite the push and reliance on dashboard reporting and other magical numbers, accurately measuring success relies on three key factors:

1. Focusing on and measuring what matters

2. Determining how to best measure those elements

3. Ensuring the context and value to understand what it means

Effective measurement is essential to evaluating participation in the conversation, the shift in thinking, and the change in behaviors. When the right elements are captured and reviewed, the insight vital to adjusting and improving the program speeds the pace of success. This can be accomplished by using quantitative measures, qualitative measures, or a hybrid approach.

QUANTITATIVE MEASURES

Most measurement focuses on quantitative measures—numbers presumed to be dispassionate and objective. Of course, numbers can be used to represent a variety of outcomes, leading to the oft-quoted maxim "numbers lie." Reporting numbers for numbers' sake is a waste of time. Quantitative measures are best when the basis for calculating those numbers is known. For example, reporting how many people have endured a security-awareness video and answered ten questions allows a compliance box on a form to be checked but provides no insight into efficacy. Quantitative measures must be trained to look for the signs of behavior change.

Using quantitative measures to assess behavior change

As outlined in Chapter 2, most organizations require the use of "strong passwords" and embark on a series of attempts to enforce their usage that falls short. After considering the human factors that have presented a barrier to individuals selecting and using good passwords, a new program to engage people has been adopted. But how will success be measured?

The first step is to set a baseline: the current strength of the password base. To do this, a member of the security team could (with permission) run a program designed to break passwords against all or a sample of the passwords. There is, of course, a caveat: if the organization already uses technology across all systems to enforce a strong password, this specific factor may be misleading. The results of this test form a baseline, as measured by:

- Number of passwords not conforming to policy
- Number or percentage of passwords "broken" within a specific timeframe that is deemed to be substandard. Use five minutes as a starting point, and adjust the threshold based on actual performance
- Number of passwords that withstood the entire simulated attack

Incorporating the number of help desk calls for password resets into the baseline is also useful. If those numbers are not currently being tracked, it might be useful to start tracking them at the beginning of the project to measure how password behaviors—including the need to reset forgotten passwords—are changing. In the event the password strength is moot due to the technology, then working to capture an understanding of the total number of required passwords and evidence of how many are being written down (in an easily defined sample) will be more important, and telling.

Once the new and improved training has been rolled out, the same process used to create the baseline can be repeated to measure the change. The program demonstrates success if the updated passwords take longer to break, and are overall more resistant to the attack. It is doubly successful—and saves money—if password reset calls to the help desk decrease. If not, then rather than declaring the training a failure (and resorting to blaming), a qualitative assessment can be completed to gain a better understanding of what happened and how the training can be improved. This test can be run on a periodic basis, with approval, and used as a measure of behavior change relative to password and other elements.

Focus on trend lines

Organizations are dynamic; static numbers that capture a moment in time provide limited value. Over time, however, a series of static measurements can be plotted to represent the trend. The trends reveal important insight on where to focus additional effort. Reviewing trends against expectations helps to improve the overall process of managing people, information, and risk. When the trend moves counter to expectations, it is often necessary to investigate further to uncover important information or reset expectations.

Trends are valuable when assessing website traffic. Organizations often focus resources and energy on assessing the metrics and trends of their external websites. However, the same approach to assessing internal websites and employee portals provides keen insight into the interests, challenges, and behaviors of the individuals of the organization. For example, understanding where on the portal people go, where they spend their time, and what part of the company they come from, all provide insights and form the basis for trends that can be studied.

This approach can also be used to track the effectiveness of different efforts. Rather than just ensuring someone completes online training to meet a requirement, it is more powerful to assess the usage and popularity of different training programs and resources. By learning how long people spent completing the training, looking at differences within different departments of the company and which elements are used—and which are ignored—resources can be allocated more efficiently to address the challenges of the individuals.

Timing is everything

When building trends and assessing numbers, it is important to understand when the information was collected—and what events may be influencing the results. Usage of an employee portal may spike when an important announcement is e-mailed to the entire company. Armed with an understanding that the e-mail is likely to produce a spike in activity sets expectations and helps to analyze the resulting activity:

- The e-mail explains the spike in activity; understanding the size of the increase in usage may be important as well as how long the increased usage lasts.
- Comparing the number of visits against the number of e-mails sent potentially demonstrates the effectiveness of the e-mail.
- Knowing when the e-mail was sent allows a trend to be established assessing—in rough terms—when people click on the link relative to when the e-mail was sent. This is useful to understand how and when people process internal messages.

These numbers, in context, also form another trend: each message can be compared to others to determine if some are more effective than others. This is a loose measurement at best and can easily be influenced by other factors; regardless, the context and trends of measurement yield insights that help develop the "story" behind the numbers that lead to more effective decision-making.

The power in this approach is the ability to drive the focus of qualitative measures—when something defies expectation, a qualitative assessment may be in order. That assessment may reveal subtle issues, or the outright failure of an effort to meet the needs of the users. Shifting the effectiveness of measurement often requires a learning curve in both assessing and interpreting the numbers. Do not be alarmed if the initial results suggest more failure than was reported using more conventional methods. As the Strategy to Protect Information begins to deliver results, this will be a temporary situation but an important baseline. Over time, the information trend lines will yield accurate insights into the success of the program.

QUALITATIVE MEASURES

Qualitative measures provide context; they bring numbers to life and reveal the "story." Although some qualitative measures can be complicated and costly to gather, employing less formal methods reduces the cost while providing the context necessary to make effective decisions. One such low-cost, high-value qualitative measure is simply to speak with individuals and ask them about their experiences. Because conversations and communication are central to the ability of an organization to manage risk more effectively, these conversations are a natural extension of that process.

Direct and honest conversations—with no pretense and no agenda—quickly shed light on how the program is working. Engaging in informal qualitative measurement requires that you simply walk around and ask probing, open-ended questions. The key is to be present and to foster a safe environment where people will naturally share their emotions and experiences. If they perceive they are being assessed, measured, or studied by a company superior, they will often provide feedback of little value.

The more engaged in the conversation, the more accurate the results. Success comes not from asking questions but by focusing on the person telling the story. This process, when effective, is about the conversation. This is an opportunity to ask about challenges, feelings, and actions. Successes can be celebrated. Listening, asking about fears and concerns, and validating them become essential. The human experience is based on story; engaging users in active conversations—especially when guided through quantitative measures—provides a richness of detail that yields the context to the numbers required to assess programs and make effective decisions.

HYBRID APPROACH

Numbers are powerful. Stories are powerful. The hybrid approach to combining quantitative and qualitative measurement yields the most accurate and useful results. Good quality results will reveal the "story behind the numbers," and good quantitative results will direct where qualitative measures need to be used.

The hybrid approach is valuable when assessing security training and awareness because most compliance regulations require annual training. To be effective, however, the training needs to be engaging and focused on supporting people as they change their mindsets and behaviors. In these cases, reviewing only completion statistics is not telling the whole picture. To be effective, it would be more useful to review the available training solutions, and then compare not only completion rates but also the time spent completing the different courses. Equally interesting would be learning how many courses were repeated and then digging deeper to understand why. These patterns are generally ripe for further explanation in a way that only a quality assessment can deliver.

It is important to ensure that good information is being collected. In my experience, the best way to do so is to use a combination of quantitative and qualitative measures—relying on both numbers and context. Good decisions can only be made when the context is clear and useful. Good decisions come from good information. Good instincts are developed with clear understanding and continued exposure to a range of experiences. Effective leaders routinely engage their people to understand the impact of their decisions and improve their ability to lead.

Part Three

9 | Extending the Conversation: Rewards Beyond Protecting Information

"The true spirit of conversation consists more in bringing out the cleverness of others than in showing a great deal of it yourself."

—*La Bruyere*[47]

THE KEY TO PROTECTING INFORMATION IS TO BLEND THE management of people, information, and risk. The Strategy to Protect Information is focused on engaging individuals in a systematic way that not only informs and improves the ability to manage risk but guides better personal action. Central to the success of this approach is the conversation. A dialogue—where listening is as important as speaking and sharing—enables the growth through participation that results in higher quality of information, understanding, the ability to manage that information, and to act. The advantage to this approach is that the

conversation can be extended—beyond protecting information—
to reap additional rewards, including:

- The "alignment" of the organization
- Improved revenue opportunities
- Reduction of costs and waste

ACHIEVE BUSINESS ALIGNMENT, GAIN EFFICIENCY

"Business alignment" is the challenge where the technology
and operations of the organization, often considered silos vying
for power, are streamlined in a way that more naturally supports the business needs driving the organization. The idea is
to develop a more efficient organization; often, the reality of
alignment efforts is the appearance of alignment while problems fester and grow. Extending the conversation started to
protect information engages individuals, draws on their experiences, and reaches the desired efficiency more effectively than
the common approach of proclamation—a top-down, one-way
communication.

The goal of alignment sometimes introduces a natural fear
of change where people are unsure of their "place" in the organization, resulting in actions that hoard knowledge in a defensive
posture. From this perspective, the resulting push to align technology, operations, and the business is sometimes perceived as a
loss of power for the people involved—and certainly the technology team. The natural reaction to change, especially change
expected to reduce power, is to resist—creating strife. This presents an opportunity to extend the conversation and explore the
roles and experiences of individuals.

Here are three ways to use conversations to guide this
process and improve the results:

1. The blended team has the opportunity to reach a common
   understanding on the actual mission, vision, and purpose of
   the effort and company.

2. Individuals engaged in facilitated conversations are able to seek out similarities, explore differences, and establish a common ground for success.

3. By sharing their view of their job, their "aha moments"—the situations and experiences that taught them—and asking questions, individuals gain insights to themselves and others.

These conversations help people gain appreciation for each other and their contributions, and a clearer understanding of roles in the organization. When people feel valued and safe—when they are empowered and enabled—they are more likely to engage with their colleagues and share ideas and information. Through shared experiences and successful interactions, they are more willing to work together and help each other. As the conversation progresses and relationships improve, less tension and competition leads to more focus on meeting the goals and the needs of the organization.

As the internal struggle is reduced, the resulting relationships also foster improvement of "institutional" knowledge that allows problems to be solved more effectively and in consistent, but evolving, ways. As a result of shifting the conversation a bit, individuals understand and participate in the same goals, each to the best of his or her abilities and roles in a way that reduces the silos and improves the overall alignment of the organization.

IMPROVED REVENUE OPPORTUNITY

It's not often that a book examining how to improve security, commonly regarded as a cost center, reveals a pathway to improved company revenue. Yet with focus and careful continuation of the conversation, the opportunities to increase revenue are improved in three key ways:

1. By focusing on what matters most to the organization

2. By engaging and empowering employees to share ideas and insights

3. By creating an empowered front line that provides better service and builds better relationships

Focus on what matters most

The strategy guides organizations to an improved understanding of their information—the lifeblood of the organization. This process helps to build a more complete picture of the organization, including the vital role information plays. This often reveals energy and resources being spent in ways that are not core to the organization. Focusing the conversation on these elements allows everyone to reach a common understanding of why this is not efficient. Additionally, it presents an opportunity to share the leadership perspectives and "aha moments." This offers organizations a pathway to focus on their core value, to strengthen it, and to improve their offerings to the marketplace. This may mean fewer projects are started and fewer solutions offered with the trade-off of more focus and higher success. Increasing the focus on the core elements of success for the organization works to improve efficiency and, through it, profitability.

Participation encourages ideas and solutions

Better information leads to better decisions. Organizations generally exist to provide a product or service of value to others. Empowering users and welcoming their participation allows an organization to benefit from their ideas, insights, passions, and experiences. Capturing and distilling this wealth of information often reveals the path to improved revenue and marketplace differentiation. People want to do their jobs—but most people also want the chance to contribute to the success of the overall organization. The strategy recognizes and engages people in that rewarding practice.

The frontline of success

Individuals that take responsibility for their actions tend to be more aware of the consequences of their actions. Client-facing team members who take pride in their actions are more inclined to present the energy, compassion, and image that leaves customers feeling valued. More importantly, providing a different and positive experience is noteworthy today—it is different than what people expect, and it will get talked about. It is easier to keep a customer than to earn a new one and happy customers lead to more customers at a lower acquisition cost.

PROTECTING THE BOTTOM LINE

Protecting or improving the bottom line can be as dramatic—and important—as increasing revenue. As a result, many organizations are being tasked to do more, with less budget and time. It is important to ensure the team is working together on this front. No question—this aspect of the conversation is fundamental to the Strategy to Protect Information—easily extended to focus a bit more on the challenges, opportunities, and experiences of the collective team. This enhanced aspect of the conversation plays an important role in working to reduce waste and enabling organizations to do more with less. Specifically, the conversation can be used to protect the bottom line in five key ways:

1. Guide the selection of projects and technologies that represent the greatest value in terms of impact and real protections to critical information.

2. Develop useful and accurate requirements, set accurate project scope, and define the elements for project success.

3. Engage people and harness their abilities to maximize efficiency without creating additional compression; reduce the cost of the project, increase the success, and ease acceptance.

4. Implement solutions and technologies matched to the needs of people—and engaging them in the process—that cost less to implement, and require less training and less to maintain (because people will actually be able to use them).

5. Help individuals take responsibility and action. People who are engaged and are practicing good situational awareness are more likely to spot problems and take action.

The result is a situation where people act in their own self-interest, but where that interest is closely aligned with the best interest of the organization. Extending the conversations requires only slight tweaks, additional focus, or a commitment to engaging in more thorough and enlightening discussions. The result of this commitment is efficiency with the opportunity for improved revenue and reduced costs without needing to change anyone or force them to learn a new approach that creates another burden. Instead, the collective knowledge of individuals is harnessed to make more informed decisions that provide benefit at a personal and organizational level.

10 | Reducing the Cost of Compliance

"Efficiency is concerned with doing things right. Effectiveness is doing the right things."
— *Peter F. Drucker*[48]

FROM DECEMBER OF 2007 UNTIL MARCH OF 2008, HANNAFORD Supermarkets failed to protect 4.2 million credit and debit card numbers—1,800 had been used fraudulently at the time the breach was disclosed.[49] As the details of the breach came to light, Hannaford explained the company was compliant with the Payment Card Industry (PCI) regulations—and had even been recertified during the period of the attack. The attack did not involve the loss of a laptop or the compromise of stored customer information; software loaded onto 300 servers compromised the information during the point-of-sale process and shipped the card numbers overseas.[50]

Hannaford learned the hard way that compliance does not provide security. The success and failure of compliance requirements is an area of constant debate—and struggle. Success in meeting compliance objectives comes when individuals are empowered and enabled to participate in the process. No single solution will protect against all attacks. However, in Hannaford's case, an alert employee taking personal responsibility would have likely noticed the server compromise and taken action to prevent or reduce the problem before it grew.

COMPLIANCE IS NOT A COMMODITY

Compliance is considered by many to be a burden, a cost of doing business that needs to be quickly addressed and "solved." Organizations expecting a quick fix are lured by the siren call of compliance vendors promising quick and easy compliance with comprehensive, product-based solutions. The decision to purchase compliance as a commodity is generally regarded as a safe approach. Buying a solution provides evidence of the effort—whether a blinking light on a device or a report generated by software, "proof" is available that action has been taken. This approach works to provide a buffer for the decision makers if the approach fails to work as planned; they can blame and pressure the vendor to produce results. For many organizations, this approach will yield *some* benefit at the expense of efficiently addressing challenges and improving how the organization protects information.

This "solutions-oriented" approach stems from a belief that the solution to the human problem we face is rooted in technology alone and fails to develop and address comprehensive requirements. Without considering the role people play in the solution—with the technology—these solutions are often presented and implemented in a way that creates a burden, evoking the human response to pain explained in Chapter 2. Without being matched to the needs of the organization and guided to success in a way that gains the support of users, many of these solutions struggle or fail during implementation and operation. The resulting frustration causes the mass outcry that "compliance" is a flop that wastes time, money, and resources, and makes no difference.

This reactionary approach creates three unintended consequences:

1. This is an expensive way to address compliance. Treating each regulation as a new project, satisfying "compliance" with one does not necessarily equate with compliance for the next.

2. In addition to being more costly, this reactionary approach creates a higher level of organizational pain as people are asked to compress more into their schedules.

3. This creates a condition known as *Security Theater*: the appearance of security and compliance while the actual risk persists—or, worse, grows as a result of a new burden on the workforce and the lack of attention paid to a problem thought to be solved.

Compliance is not a commodity. Each organization needs to assess how information is collected, stored, processed, and protected to ensure efficiency and compliance. *Satisfying and declaring compliance does not equate with security.* Protecting information in a way that is efficient and demonstrated—as outlined in the Strategy to Protect Information—can lead to true compliance. This approach allows organizations to demonstrate compliance with a wide range of initiatives without the need for drastic and disruptive changes.

LESSONS LEARNED FROM BANKING REGULATIONS

In October 2005, the United States Federal Financial Institutions Examination Council (FFIEC) updated guidance to financial institutions on the need to improve authentication of customers. From the press release:

> *"This guidance, which replaces the FFIEC's Authentication in an* Electronic Banking Environment *issued in 2001, does not endorse any particular technology. This guidance specifically addresses the need for risk-based assessment, customer awareness, and financial institutions' implementation of*

appropriate risk mitigation strategies including security measures to reliably authenticate customers accessing their financial institutions' Internet-based services.[51]

The drivers for this guidance were simple and clear—as consumers were growing concerned with using the Internet for banking transactions, the industry needed to take steps to ensure the safety of online transactions and protect the privacy and identity of customers. This was not an effort that pitted institution against institution; rather, this was a needed effort on the part of the industry to maintain and restore confidence in their profitable and important online properties. I had the opportunity to partner with an investment bank to study the process and available solutions and share insights with the industry.

In light of a rising concern for financial institutions, the FFIEC[52] guidance required each organization to:

1. Assess high-risk online banking applications for the need for stronger authentication mechanisms.

2. Based on the assessment, select a solution to provide multi-layer authentication (note: this is weaker than the multi-factor initially proposed).

3. Implement and test the solution.

4. Educate consumers on how to use the new solution.

5. Monitor the solution for fraud.

Rather than mandate a specific approach or technology solution, a reasonable process to first assess and then improve client authentication was presented. In fact, if an organization, through a reasonable and documented risk assessment, could demonstrate there was no risk to its clients, no changes would need to be made.

Our research, which consisted of online surveys, telephone interviews, and literature reviews, identified two trends:

- A large majority selected the solution before conducting a risk assessment. For many, this was based on the recommendation of third-party providers.

- Those who conducted a risk assessment did so more as a perfunctory exercise than a true analysis.

As with other compliance directives, the need to meet this guidance was taken seriously. Yet most organizations struggled to satisfy the requirements and integrate them into a final solution. As we continued our research, we learned that user education was not being actively considered by many organizations. A common complaint fielded during a panel conversation was the lack of an enforced singular solution; rather than following the process in the interest of selecting a solution matched to the needs of the organization and the protection of the clients, this regulation posed a problem that demanded a quick solution.

Lessons learned

This experience revealed three key points that must be considered when addressing compliance:

1. Many organizations, when faced with a new compliance initiative, seek what appears to be the shortest path. In the case of the FFIEC guidance, however, some of the banks we worked with admitted their initial solution would need to be changed in the coming year. What appears to be the shortest path to compliance often is not.

2. Regulations and legislation often leave the final decision to the organization. This is good. Regulations take time to bring to bear and need to be designed in a way that is solution agnostic; when regulations start to stipulate specific requirements, unintended consequences run the risk of destroying a

good intention. However, some regulations do point to additional *guidance* that often suggests technologies or solutions to consider. When working to comply with regulations, the additional guidance is a valuable asset to understand the intention behind the regulation and the range of solutions that were considered when drafting it. This often provides insights to guide the final solution.

3. Organizations that focus less on compliance for compliance's sake and instead adopt a strategy and mindset to protect information are often challenged to incorporate additional compliance requirements quickly with little additional effort.

USING THE STRATEGY TO IMPROVE COMPLIANCE

Regardless of the challenge being solved, *solutions follow requirements.* The implementation of the strategy provides the information and guidance to assess and document requirements effectively. From this approach, the most critical information and resources will be addressed efficiently—and in a way that meets the needs of compliance objectives. The strategy reduces the cost of compliance management by focusing on meeting compliance *through* the protection of information. The shift in mindset and the way people protect information provide an easier and less expensive path to demonstrating compliance.

The bottom line on compliance is that is not a commodity good, but it does not have to be a burden or expensive. The Strategy to Protect Information can not only improve the selection and implementation of the technologies and tools to support compliance but reduce the cost of ongoing compliance management by eliminating waste and engaging people in the process.

11 | Outsource with Security and Success

"I don't care if you start with (Gov. Jim) Doyle or somebody else, but somebody's not doing their job . . ."

> —Jane Marvin, a Wisconsin
> resident affected by an error of an
> outsource provider to the State of
> Wisconsin[53]

DESPITE THE RISING POPULARITY AND EFFECTIVENESS OF outsourcing operations to a third party, the protection of information cannot be overlooked. EDS, a third–party provider responsible for processing Medicaid information in Wisconsin, printed the social security numbers of four hundred eighty-five thousand people on the address label of a mailing. A *recipient* caught the mistake—*after* two hundred and sixty thousand had already been mailed. Ultimately, EDS accepted responsibility, agreed to pay for credit monitoring for those affected, and fired the person deemed responsible for the mistake.[54] Yet the state government took the brunt of the anger from many residents.

Rather than attempting to layer additional burdens on a somewhat complex effort to outsource, the Strategy to Protect Information, relying on a process-driven approach, guides the establishment and operation of outsourcing arrangements to improve the end result and help ensure the protection of information. Increased participation and accuracy of information informs decision-making and ensures focus is kept on the elements that matter: to bring the biggest impact in the most efficient way. This brings at least three benefits:

1. Improves the quality of information on which decisions are based—improving the pace and quality of the results.

2. Guides the evaluation of the vendors and ensures a more complete and accurate understanding of their capabilities, including the roles individuals play in protecting information.

3. Integrates the solution into current operations more effectively by engaging the very people affected/benefited by the relationship.

Trusting a third party to protect the information of the organization is an inherently risky proposition. It is challenging enough to engage people compressed by hectic schedules and increasing demands to take responsibility and shift their mindset to one of protecting information. The ability to exert that influence and engage with the third party is naturally limited, increasing the likelihood that the third party is more disconnected from the information and divorced from the consequences. The more thorough the assessment and understanding of how, beyond contractual agreements, the partner protects information is critical.

EXTEND THE STRATEGY: EVALUATION CONSIDERATIONS

Outsourced arrangements need to be considered in the context of how people do their jobs. If they seem too good to be true, they probably will create a condition that encourages people to take shortcuts and otherwise reduce the protection of information.

It may be helpful to review contractual agreements with the vendor in a setting that allows the agreements to be tested and adjusted to provide the necessary results without unnecessary risk. When extending the strategy to evaluating the outsourcing relationship, the same *approach* is used, but some of the questions may change. This approach helps to focus on:

1. Understanding how the employees of the vendor use and protect information; this is as important as assessing vendor policies and technical controls, if not more so.

2. Assessing how the vendor protects information—theirs and that of the organization.

3. Evaluating the ability to work with the vendor to reach a mutual understanding of language, process, and expectations through shared experience; this is absolutely key to a healthy and efficient relationship.

Here are some additional considerations to be incorporated into the elements of the strategy implementation when evaluating different outsourced relationships. The specifics of each will evolve, based on the needs of the organization, through conversation and experience.

Culture
Developing an understanding of the culture of the outsource provider is important. Culture extends to not only the country and region of origin, but also to how the employees act and are expected to act. Many outsourcing relationships encounter surprise and friction over cultural differences not previously explored.

Policies and procedures
Nearly every organization is expected to have a comprehensive set of policies and procedures. To be effective and useful, a review

of policies, procedures, and controls must also include how people apply them in the course of doing their jobs. This requires an assessment to gauge the effectiveness of those programs and the engagement of the employees. External and partner assessments are time consuming; to be effective, the constraint of being done "yesterday" needs to be lifted. Making the wrong decision can often lead to a breach.

A potential snag in the process is the situation where the policies of the vendor are either more lax or the review team draws the conclusion that the comprehensive policies are not well known or followed. There is no simple way to address the situation. In some cases, this will be an important selection criteria and the vendor is excluded. More likely, however, is the need for additional negotiation—central to the strategy—and special arrangements that govern the data of the organization. The drawback to this approach is the challenge of the vendor actually to enforce and protect the data to the more stringent standard. The relationship between the organization and vendor will dictate a solution that is acceptable, implemented, and tested.

Hiring, training, and user education

It is important to understand how people are hired, including screening and background checks. Useful information includes understanding the process, including who conducts the checks and what the background check includes. After comfort is gained with the hiring process, ask about turnover, retention, and employee satisfaction. Inquire and observe training and other user education sessions. People are key to the protection of information and warrant careful consideration when making the outsourcing choice.

A key driver for outsourcing—especially security operations—is the challenge in finding qualified personnel for the organization. It is entirely possible that other organizations, including outsource partners, share the same challenge. Part of the assessment process and agreement needs to document the required skills and experience clearly and a method for verifying these skills.

Risk tolerance level

Managing risk on the efficient frontier requires a clear understanding of risk tolerance. This means understanding the risk tolerance of the organization and the vendor. This is important in figuring out where the vendor fits in the overall risk management strategy. There is no hard and fast rule that the risk tolerance of the provider should be more or less than that of the organization, only the understanding of the tolerance they have for risk and the related actions they take to manage that risk. Effective and healthy agreements that benefit the organization are developed on a clear and accurate description of expectations and the risk, risk tolerance, and processes to assess and verify compliance with the agreed-upon practices.

Controls and incident handling

From a risk perspective, the third party may carry some or all of the liability when agreeing to field some or all of the operations, but the third party cannot absorb the fiduciary duty to act. Controls can be operational and technical. Most companies are proficient at reviewing technical controls, but the operational controls that affect people must also be considered. In the event there is a problem, it is crucial to understand how it will be handled and what actions will be taken. It is important to develop a level of comfort and a set of controls that reinforce that comfort. In the words of Ronald Reagan, "Trust, but verify."

The larger the scope or the more sensitive the information the vendor will be handling, the more complete this process needs to be. How a vendor handles an incident ranges from direct questions to mock drills and even external tests—with and without notice. The method used to test the vendor should be included in the final agreement.

Disaster recovery

Fiduciary duty continues with the organization after the agreement is signed, and extends to manmade and natural disasters. This goes beyond simply understanding the vendor's plans, if any, for disaster recovery. It is important to assess the region and climate of the vendor to understand the propensity for disasters and other events that could adversely impact the organization, including natural disasters, political turmoil, communications (for example, when the undersea cables are damaged), and the data protection laws.

In some areas, disasters happen with a frequency and intensity that could cause a disruption of days or possibly weeks. What is the recourse in the event something goes horribly wrong?

Prior and current operational experience

Do they have the operational experience required to provide business value and protect information? Many outsource providers have developed a reputation in a specific niche, which makes them attractive for outsourcing. The protection of information is often ignored or only lightly treated, because the business objective often is perceived as more important. When outsourcing, the potential gains can be erased and penalties incurred if information is not protected properly and in accordance with any prevailing regulations. Requiring proof of experience is important, as is asking about previous problems and handling. An organization that claims "no problems" is either unaware or not forthcoming and warrants closer inspection or removal from the selection process.

Assurance and validation

How will assurance be provided that the controls are being used properly and the information entrusted to the outsource partner is being protected?

Consider that the actions of the third party are considered the actions of the organization. Outsourcing rarely removes liability, especially in the court of public opinion. There is no substitute for appropriate due diligence. Following the strategy and addressing these considerations will help to avoid the situation where the agreement looks great on paper and suffers in practice. Extending the process-driven Strategy to Protect Information is an effective way to combat that curse of outsourcing, but it requires an equal commitment from all parties.

THE KEY TO SUCCESS: STRONG RELATIONSHIPS

The most effective and successful outsourcing arrangements share a single trait—a strong relationship. The strategy presents an effective approach to forge relationships with mutually understood language and common experiences that lead to mutual and reasonable expectations. Successful arrangements include written agreements that clearly spell out responsibilities, actions, and penalties. This includes an investment in ensuring the language used is mutually understood. Responsibilities and expectations need to be reasonable and enforceable—operationally and legally. It needs to include a clear understanding of how performance will be measured and controls audited.

Success boils down to active participation, active review, and active ongoing engagement. Clear, effective, and continual communication is necessary. Once the agreement is reached, review mutual experiences on a regular basis. This will work to enrich the relationship further and prevent future problems. Celebrate and focus on the successes as well as the challenges, but when addressing the challenges, keep an eye toward a mutual remedy. Relationships that become very one-sided are poised for failure unless the fee paid is substantial. Document the lessons learned and update contracts and the other agreements as necessary.

12 | Final Thoughts: Courage to Act

"Courage is contagious. When a brave man takes a stand, the spines of others are often stiffened."
—Billy Graham[55]

EMBRACING THE STRATEGY TO PROTECT INFORMATION AND guiding the implementation to success take courage and dedication. In a time when people are addicted to their hyperreactive schedules and demonstrating the latest gadgets, true progress comes from a commitment to engaging in conversations designed to shift the mindsets of the people in the organization. Although change is uncomfortable for some, this book has suggested an approach that reduces the impact on people and allows the change to be implemented in gradual ways. This means the process will feel less like change and more like an improvement. As the strategy takes hold and conversations increase in both frequency and quality, participation increases and effective decision-making improves at the individual and organizational levels.

Courage is what allows a leader to serve people and ensure that they are able to meet their obligations easier, while also being able to satisfy the expectations of the organization and protect information. The boldness of these actions will be met with the potential of an improved bottom line and the ability to manage people, information, and risk on the efficient frontier. The key is to get started; even taking small steps will yield benefit. Convert initial "quick wins" into long-term success.

Although it takes courage to act, failure to act also has consequences. Identify and avoid decision paralysis. Done right, the benefits of taking these bold steps will last for years to come.

BUILD YOUR FLYWHEEL

One last analogy: Newton's first law, commonly referred to as the law of inertia, demonstrates that a body in motion will continue in motion unless another force opposes it. This principle holds true for the properly implemented Strategy to Protect Information. In fact, understanding, adapting, and implementing the Strategy to Protect Information is a lot like building a flywheel. Think of it in these five steps:

1. Learn about flywheels, develop the plans, and gather the appropriate materials and expertise. It is helpful during this stage to consult books on flywheels, flywheel experts, and engineers.

2. Once the plan and budget have been constructed, the flywheel can be built. Often, the building process includes experts and outside assistance integrated into the team. The building process is crucial; the better the design and teamwork involved, the more efficient and easier to operate the flywheel will be.

3. After the flywheel is built and tested, it needs to be started. It takes a lot of energy to get the flywheel started; the bigger the flywheel, the more energy is needed. There is a start-up cost associated with starting the wheel, and the initial momentum either comes from a concentrated internal effort, the work of skilled outsiders, or a combination of both.

4. If the flywheel was properly designed and built, maintaining the momentum and operation can be done at a fraction of the start-up cost. The flywheel is a process that requires energy and attention, but the momentum of the flywheel itself reduces that need.

5. Even the best flywheels need to be maintained. Periodic and preventative maintenance includes inspections—both internal and external—and upgrades to some of the components.

There is another important consideration to flywheels—a benefit shared by the Strategy to Protect Information. There is a movement away from the use of expensive battery back-up systems, designed to protect the computing infrastructure in the event of a power outage, and toward the use of flywheel-driven generators. Each system is different, but the principle is the same. The flywheel, once started, requires little additional power to keep the momentum going. In the event of power loss, *the flywheel continues to turn*, generating the power required to keep the computers running until the back-up generators turn on or power is restored.

Batteries can only serve the stored charge; flywheels continue the momentum. The Strategy to Protect Information is the flywheel for your information protection. Even during the times when power may not directly be applied, it will continue to operate. People will make better decisions. As Einstein suggested, this necessary change in the way people protect information requires a touch of genius and a truckload of courage.

A CAVEAT FROM NEWTON

Newton's second law of motion is known as the law of acceleration. It is mathematically expressed as $F = m \times a$. The force on an object is equal to its mass multiplied by its acceleration. When applied to the efforts of implementing the Strategy to Protect Information, force equals the effort to implement and adapt the strategy, mass represents the organization, and acceleration is the expression of movement. Movement is the sign the program is working.

In small organizations, it will take less force to move the mass, and the acceleration—or signs that the program is working—will be evident sooner. This also suggests that larger organizations will require more force in order to accelerate toward change. This can be accomplished by implementing a successful pilot, recruiting and developing champions, and being persistent. But it means more! Even the efforts of a single person have an effect; no matter how small the acceleration, the efforts of one person to apply "force"—in the spirit of the law, not in the literal sense—have an impact on the mass of the organization. Even if not visible, change is happening.

In this law, Newton did not address energy exchange—the simple and easy-to-prove aspect that in order to keep the mass moving, force will need to be applied continually. The Strategy to Protect Information is a mindset, a plan of action—a process-driven approach—that cannot be applied once and forgotten; it needs to be incorporated into the organization. Even a flywheel will eventually stop. So, although the strategy is designed to be *easier* to operate over time with less energy and resources, it still requires attention. Newton's second law, then, holds a powerful corollary: things may not happen the same way twice.

In terms of Newton's law, as changes in mass, friction, and other external elements change, the force required and acceleration experienced will change. In terms of the Strategy to Protect Information, no two paths will be the same, and each application (or each round) of the process will be different. The inherent flexibility of the strategy readily adapts to this corollary. This corollary is freedom—the freedom to take this strategy and test it, customize it, adapt it, and claim it. There is no right way, no wrong way, and no two ways will be precisely the same. Yet the framework and distilled principles will remain intact.

About the Author

Michael Santarcangelo is a human catalyst*. An expert who speaks on information protection—including compliance, privacy and awareness—Michael energizes and inspires his audiences to change the way they protect information.

Michael is known for delivering simple and effective strategies that get results. He connects with audiences in a way that makes security relevant, easy to understand, and achievable! With wit and clarity, he freely shares unique insights, innovative approaches and effective solutions that are informed by both experience and research.

As the voice of optimism in an industry of doomsayers, Michael provides guidance to executives to defend their organization against breaches while discovering how to increase revenue, protect the bottom line, and efficiently manage people, information, and risk. He provides solutions that shift thinking and change behaviors.

Michael is currently taking his message of optimism on the road with the Campaign Across America, a cross-country speaking tour to guide individuals and businesses to greater security.

---

* *A substance, usually present in small amounts, that increases the rate of a reaction without being consumed in the process.*

EFFICIENT SOLUTIONS FOR INFORMATION PROTECTION

Michael has pioneered unique services to engage people in the process of information protection. The security salon (www.securitysalon.com) facilitates the exchange of ideas in a way that allows people to learn and apply their knowledge for immediate results and program success. The Security Catalyst Show is an audio series available on podcast in which Michael shares powerful and productive insights. The Security Catalyst Community is a supportive online environment where security professionals from around the world come together to improve the way they practice information security.

INDUSTRY CREDENTIALS

A full member of the National Speakers Association, Michael was named one of The 59 Top Influencers in IT Security in 2007 (www.itsecurity.com), and was selected to serve on the Symantec Advisory Council. He actively supports various industry associations and remains a secure member of the FBI InfraGard program.

Michael is a graduate of Cornell University. When not traveling North America in their RV, Michael and his family reside in upstate New York.

Additional Resources and Support

The Strategy to Protect Information is a dynamic and powerful approach to addressing the challenges faced by business today. Consider engaging Michael Santarcangelo—The Security Catalyst—to energize, inspire, and guide your team, organization, or event to success by shifting thinking and changing the way people protect information.

Call 1.800.996.8351 to check availability and get started today, or visit www.securitycatalyst.com or www.intothebreach.com for more details.

SPEAKING

Change the way your group protects information by engaging the security catalyst. Build on the book—with even more examples and case studies, carefully chosen for your specific needs. Fully customized and designed to engage and inspire, Michael gets the results needed to effectively manage people, information, and risk.

EXECUTIVE BOOK CLUB

Take your team through the book—expertly guided by the author. Engage, energize, and inspire your team with fresh thinking and the tools to change. Shift their thinking, change behavior.

The book club sessions are tailored to your exacting needs and allow for plenty of conversation.

SECURITY SALON: PROTECTING INFORMATION PROGRAM
Implement the book—following the tenets of the book ... and beyond. Through the innovative security salon—get answers, explanations, and the support needed get results when managing people, information, and risk.

ONSITE IMPLEMENTATION AND SUPPORT
Work with Michael to enhance and extend the Strategy to Protect Information to address the challenges of your organization. Build an awareness program that changes the way people protect information, enhance training, develop policy, or tackle the challenges you face armed with a Strategy that gets results.

Endnotes

1. In Drew Pearson and Robert S. Allen, "How the President Works," *Harper's*, June 1936.
2. http://www.finextra.com/fullstory.asp?id=14395
   http://www.finextra.com/fullstory.asp?id=13988
   http://www.nytimes.com/2005/06/21/business/21card.html
   http://www.securityfocus.com/brief/16
   http://www.ftc.gov/opa/2006/02/cardsystems_r.shtm
   http://www.wired.com/science/discoveries/news/2005/06/67980
3. http://www.freenewmexican.com/news/64747.html
   http://www.freenewmexican.com/news/69474.html
   http://www.pogo.org/p/environment/eo-losalamos.html
   http://www.computerworld.com/action/article.do?command=view
   ArticleBasic&articleId=299200&intsrc=news_list
   http://dailybruin.ucla.edu/news/2007/jul/16/uc_fined_los_alamos_
   breach/
4. http://www.privacyatchoicepoint.com/
   http://www.privacyrights.org/ar/ChronDataBreaches.htm
   http://www.ftc.gov/opa/2006/01/choicepoint.shtm
   http://www.ftc.gov/choicepoint
   http://www.scmagazineus.com/ChoicePoint-settles-lawsuit-over-2005-
   breach/article/104649/
   http://www.consumeraffairs.com/news04/2008/01/choicepoint_settle.
   html
5. http://www.deloitte.com/dtt/article/0%2C1002%2Ccid%25253D182733%
   2C00.html
   Enterprise@Risk: 2007 Privacy & Data Protection Survey.
6. http://www.privacyrights.org/ar/ChronDataBreaches.htm
7. http://attrition.org/dataloss/
   http://www.privacyrights.org/ar/ChronDataBreaches.htm

8. *The Confessions Survey: Office Workers Reveal Everyday Behavior That Places Sensitive Information at Risk,* RSA, November 2007.
9. http://www.consumeraffairs.com/news04/2006/11/starbucks_data. html
   http://authentium.blogspot.com/2007/05/60-of-enterprise-data-on-laptops.html
   http://www.numbrx.net/2006/11/05/starbucks-loses-employee-data/
   http://www.starbucks.com/aboutus/pressdesc.asp?id=716
10. http://www.adamdodge.com/esi/yir_2007
11. http://www.computerworld.com/securitytopics/security/story/0,10801,108268,00.html
12. http://www.adamdodge.com/esi/print_out_containing_21_000_student_records_stolen
13. *Emile: or, Treatise on Education, 4, 1762,* tr. Barbar Foxley, 1911.
14. http://www.nytimes.com/2007/12/30/business/30digi.html?ex=1356670800&en=bafd771bdcae2594&ei=5124&partner=permalink&exprod=permalink
15. http://newsvote.bbc.co.uk/mpapps/pagetools/print/news.bbc.co.uk/2/hi/business/6976084.stm
   http://www.ilo.org/public/english/employment/strat/kilm/index.htm
16. http://epic.org/privacy/vatheft/
17. *The Confessions Survey: Office Workers Reveal Everyday Behavior That Places Sensitive Information at Risk,* RSA, November 2007.
18. http://breachblog.com/2008/03/03/hn.aspx
19. *The Confessions Survey: Office Workers Reveal Everyday Behavior That Places Sensitive Information at Risk,* RSA, November 2007.
20. http://www.portfolio.com/news-markets/top-5/2008/02/05/Eli-Lilly-E-Mail-to-New-York-Times
21. http://breachblog.com/2008/02/10/bjs.aspx
   http://doj.nh.gov/consumer/pdf/BJ.pdf
22. http://oit.nd.edu/policies/itstandards/strongpassword.shtml
23. http://news.bbc.co.uk/2/hi/technology/3639679.stm
24. *Maxims, 633, 1665,* tr. Leonard Tancock, 1959.
25. http://www.consumeraffairs.com/news04/2007/08/breaches_retirees.html
26. http://www.consumeraffairs.com/news04/2007/08/verisign_breach.html
27. http://www.utica.edu/academic/institutes/cimip/publications/index.cfm?action=form&paper=6
28. http://www.symantec.com/business/theme.jsp?themeid=threatreport

29. http://www.news.com/Could-your-laptop-be-worth-millions/2100-1029_3-6032177.html
30. *The Confessions Survey: Office Workers Reveal Everyday Behavior That Places Sensitive Information at Risk,* RSA, November 2007.
31. http://www.ocregister.com/news/kim-numbers-affairs-1924451-security-social
32. *Stride Toward Freedom,* 11, 1958.
33. http://www.digitaljournal.com/article/249311/Angry_Employee_Deletes_7_Years_Worth_of_Data
    http://www.shortnews.com/start.cfm?id=67997
    http://www.firstcoastnews.com/news/local/news-article.aspx?storyid=100625
34. *The Business of Data Breach,* publication by Ponemon Institute, May 15, 2007, p 2.
35. *The Business of Data Breach,* publication by Ponemon Institute, May 15, 2007, p 4.
36. Wason, P. C.; Shapiro, D. (1966). "Reasoning," in Foss, B. M., *New Horizons in Psychology.* Harmondsworth: Penguin.
    http://www.psych.ucsb.edu/research/cep/socex/wason.htm
    http://www.psych.ucsb.edu/research/cep/socex/howmindsees.htm
    http://coglab.wadsworth.com/experiments/WasonSelection.shtml
37. http://www.newyorker.com/reporting/2008/03/03/080303fa_fact_holt?currentPage=all
38. http://online.wsj.com/public/article/SB118911962698519942-kbt-1Of1fGbvLlSHGpaHeXGZqwnM_20081113.html
39. http://www.worsleyschool.net/science/files/toiletpaper/history.html
40. *Educational Security Incidents (ESI) Year in Review—2007.* Adam Dodge. p5.
41. http://www.moneychimp.com/articles/risk/efficient_frontier.htm
    http://www.riskglossary.com/link/efficient_frontier.htm
42. Letter to Baron von Stein, 14 January 1814. In J. F. C. Fuller, *The Conduct of War,* 3.3, 1961.
43. "Letter of Instruction Number 1," 6 March 1944, appendix (D) to *War As I Knew It,* 1947.
44. http://csrc.nist.gov/publications/fips/fips199/FIPS-PUB-199-final.pdf
45. In John Peers, comp., *1,001 Logical Laws,* p. 177, 1979.
46. *Green Water, Green Sky,* 1, 1959.
47. "Of Society and of Conversation" (16), *The Character, 1688.* Tr. Henri van Laun, 1929.
48. *Management: Tasks, Responsibilities, Practices,* 2, 1974, abr., 1977.
49. http://www.boston.com/business/ticker/2008/03/supermarket_dat.html?p1=Well_MostPop_Emailed4

50. http://www.boston.com/news/local/articles/2008/03/28/advanced_
    tactic_targeted_grocer/?page=full
51. http://www.ffiec.gov/press/pr101205.htm
52. http://www.ffiec.gov/pdf/authentication_guidance.pdf
53. http://www.jsonline.com/story/index.aspx?id=705095
54. http://www.greenbaypressgazette.com/apps/pbcs.dll/article?AID=
    /20080125/GPG0101/801250712/1207/GPGnews
55. "A Time for Moral Courage," *Reader's Digest*, July 1964.

Index